THE COMPLETE KETO AIR FRYER COOKBOOK FOR BEGINNERS 2019

100+ Craveable Ketogenic Air Frying Recipes for Your Diet

by Ronda Jones

CONTENTS

INTRODUCTION

Are you trying to live a healthy and happy life? Do you want to improve your eating habits but still struggle with self-control and diets? If you answered "Yes", do not panic! You are not alone; many of us struggle with a long-term weight loss and healthy eating. With so many diets, kitchen appliances, cookbooks, and different information, it is difficult to know what to focus on.

An Air Fryer has come to solve this issue! With its exceptional and advanced technology, it will shape the future of cooking and dieting. To be healthy and happy right now does not require a lot of time, money or sacrifice. It requires just a little motivation and the right information. This unique and innovative kitchen appliance uses the power of superheated air to cook food in a specially engineered cooking basket, by providing you and your family with healthier options every day. Luckily, a modern technology improves daily lives, making it easier and better!

There is no magic wand, but remember that the right dietary regimen and persistence can do wonders! A ketogenic diet promotes healthy food choices for a lifetime; instead of following rigid dietary rules and unrealistic weight-loss goals, simply embrace good eating habits. After all, you are what you eat.

The Ketogenic Diet in a Nutshell

A ketogenic diet is low in carbohydrates and high in fats, which results in weight loss and improved health. The primary goal of a ketogenic diet is to get your body into the state of ketosis, which is a natural, metabolic state.

According to Wikipedia, ketosis is a "metabolic state in which some of the body's energy supply comes from ketone bodies in the blood, in contrast to a state of glycolysis in which blood glucose provides energy."

It means your body uses ketones for energy instead of glucose, and consequently, it becomes a fat-burner instead of a sugar-burner.

You can achieve this goal by simply avoiding carbs and eating protein food and healthy fats instead. How does that sound to you? Can you do this? No matter how easy and healthy it may be, you should follow some general rules in order to achieve the best results and stay healthy during a ketogenic diet. Since many common ingredients contain carbohydrates, it can be tricky. However, it is possible to eat low-carb food every day in the long term. When you buy groceries, read labels carefully to make sure that a certain product can fit into your low-carb diet.

Since your body needs over 45 different nutrients on a daily basis, you should follow the recommended macronutrient ratio. It means, to balance your diet, you should eat 5–10 percent of calories from carbs, 15–30 percent of calories from protein, and 60–75 percent of calories from fat.

What to eat on a ketogenic diet:

VEGETABLES – non-starchy veggies and pickled vegetables (preferably homemade).

MEAT & POULTRY – any type. The fat on the meat is also allowed.

FISH & SEAFOOD – any type. Fatty fish such as salmon, sardines or herring are a good choice.

DAIRY PRODUCTS – opt for full-fat cheese, yogurt, and milk. A cream (40% fat) and butter are great on a ketogenic diet. Be careful with skim milk as it usually contains a lot of sugar.

EGGS – poached, scrambled, deviled, boiled, fried, omelets, hard-boiled, all kinds are allowed.

NATURAL FAT – organic oil, butter, cream; feel free to experiment and try high-fat sauces such as Hollandaise sauce. Coconut oil and olive oil are the best options for everyone not only for keto dieters.

NUTS – the best options are Brazil, macadamia and pecan nuts. You can use a nut butter too, but be careful with a store-bought butter; make your own homemade peanut or almond butter.

FRUITS – you can eat berries in moderation.

DRINKS – water, regular or sparkling; black coffee with a full-fat cream (without sugar, of course); tea. For instance, if you added a sugar cube to your coffee, you can take 4 grams of carbs and that is not good for your diet. Wine is good in moderation since a serving size (about 5 ounces) contains 2 grams of carbohydrates. One cup of coconut water contains 9 grams of carbohydrates; you can always enjoy something else with no carbs at all but this is just for illustration purposes.

SWEETENERS – erythritol, monk fruit, stevia, and other sweeteners with a low glycemic index.

You cannot eat: grains rice, sugar, beans, legumes, and starchy vegetables.

Top Benefits of a Ketogenic Diet

1. **A healthy lifestyle…here we come!**

   Going into a state of ketosis not only reduces your insulin levels but it helps you control your blood sugar. When you eat lots of carbs, primarily found in pasta, bread, and sugary foods, it causes your body to produce a lot of insulin and glucose. Insulin is the chemical that helps your body turn glucose into energy. On the other hand, if you avoid carbs, your body will break down fats instead of carbs, which leads to more energy for daily activities.

   It can help you lower triglycerides that are stored in your fat cells. Nutritionists and physicians recommend eating fatty fish and healthy fats (peanut butter, avocado, seeds, and nuts) to reduce the risk of stroke. A keto diet can help reduce the symptoms of heart disease, Parkinson's disease

   Alzheimer's disease, migraines, and inflammation. Impressive!

   Here is one more advantage of a healthy diet – the more real foods you include in your diet, such as organic vegetables and pasture-raised meat, the better. The quality of your food matters so a ketogenic diet promotes whole, unprocessed food.

2. **This lifestyle boosts brain function.**

   The state of ketosis improves brain function, eliminating brain fog and lack of focus. This metabolic state balances the neurotransmitters in the brain. In addition, it improves mental focus, clarity and productivity. Due to the reduction of glucose, you will be able to reduce stress and anxiety. Added benefits of ketosis are better cognitive function and improved concentration.

3. **A natural way to lose weight.**

   As you probably already know, your body needs a constant supply of energy from the food. As mentioned above, carbs produce insulin and glucose, which causes fat to be stored in your cells instead of being burnt. When you avoid carbs, your body produces far lesser amounts of glucose and the state of ketosis kick starts! When your cells don't have access to glucose, they use fat for energy. It means that your fat cells just shrink and you can kick-start weight loss. This is also a great way to reduce excessive appetite automatically so you will need fewer calories. You will also get rid of cravings for junk food and sugary snacks.

4. **An easy way to improve energy levels and sleep better.**
Almost without exception, if you avoid carbs, your body will break down fat instead of carbs, which leads to more energy for daily activities. Moreover, researchers have found that a ketogenic dieting improves the quality of sleep naturally by enhancing slow-wave sleep.

Here are a few extra tips that might come in handy especially when you're just starting out.

- Focus on a clear protein, whole food and natural products and you'll be just fine.
- Take it easy, give yourself about two to three weeks to adjust to a diet; your body will thank you.
- Replenish electrolytes with a homemade bone broth. You can do this by simply adding salt to your drinking water as well.
- Meal planning and meal prep are vital to your long-term success on any diet, including a low-carb one.
- Stay determined – wherever you go, make sure you have ketogenic-approved food on hand. We cannot emphasize enough the importance of preparing to ensure success on a diet.
- Keep it simple by preparing meals in bulk and freeze them for the week; or you can eat the same thing for dinner a few times and pack leftovers for the next day's lunch.
- Flavor foods with seasonings instead of using sauces or gravy with flour.
- Stay hydrated. Always.
- Always consult your physician before beginning any dietary program.

Is there a foolproof system for cooking healthy, ketosis-inducing meals? Two words: AIR FRYER!

Before You Buy that Air Fryer: How it Works?

If you just could not stand the idea of avoiding fried food, but you don't like all those extra calories that you take with it, air frying may become a long-term solution for you!

The Air Fryer makes your everyday cooking convenient and healthy by using revolutionary hot air cooking technology. Besides frying, air fryers allow you to roast vegetables, bake cakes, grill steaks, and steam delicate vegetables and seafood. The Air Fryer produces meals that are exceptionally healthy, quick, and flavorful; it pushes the limits of imagination. Incredible!

What is the secret behind excellent air fried fish, chips, and cakes? How can you make healthy fried food as good as professional chefs? It is called Rapid Air Technology. The Air Fryer heats up quickly; then, hot air swirls in the specialized chamber, cooking food evenly, using a minimum amount of fat. Your food cooks in its own natural juices so it retains its natural taste, texture and nutrients. The result is perfectly cooked food that tastes good and looks great on your table. All this without having to deep fry your food in a large quantity of oil. Any food that can be cooked in an oven, microwave or toaster, can be cooked in your Air Fryer.

Thanks to an automatic temperature control, you just have to set your device and you can be assured that your food will be cooked to perfection. How does it work in practice? Spritz a removable cooking basket with a nonstick cooking spray. Place your ingredients in the cooking basket and set your desired temperature; then, wait for the buzzer to signal the end of cooking.

There are some genius cooking tips from professional chefs that will help you to get the most out of your Air Fryer.

- To keep foods from sticking to the interior of the cooking basket, simply brush the bottom and sides with a cooking oil. It is also important for an easy cleanup.
- If you want a crispy surface on your vegetables, spritz them with a nonstick oil in the cooking basket.
- Never overfill the cooking basket.
- Clean your Air Fryer after every use; wipe the outside of the Air Fryer with a moist cloth and clean the cooking basket with hot water and dish detergent.
- You can use oven-safe dishes in your Air Fryer and bake the best cakes and frittatas ever. Make sure to check with the manual before using a new bakeware.
- Make sure to test your food for doneness because cooking times vary depending on the Air Fryer model. You can use a food thermometer.
- You can prepare frozen foods in your Air Fryer machine; just make sure to follow the cooking chart.
- You can use your Air Fryer to reheat ingredients by setting the temperature to 300 degrees F for up to 10 minutes.

How You'll Benefit from an Air Fryer

1. **No grease, fewer calories.**
After detailed discussion, the International Food Research Journal concluded "The present results that the oil uptake was lower under air-frying confirming that this technique can be considered as a healthy one. Thus, this method must be practically process applied to obtain healthy fried foods."

Realistically speaking, we love the taste of fried foods but not the mess and excess fat. Studies have shown that oils release toxic chemicals at high temperatures; these toxins can be a trigger for serious health problems such as cancer, high cholesterol, diabetes, and obesity. This is a health-conscious way to cook favorite foods using olive oil, coconut oil, and butter. In comparison to deep frying, air fryers produce food with about 80 percent less fat!

2. Flavors, please!

Air frying is an exceptional way to fry foods using a hot air and it doesn't mean skimping on flavor. Thanks to the hot sealed environment, valuable nutrients are conserved and the flavors are richer and stronger. If you thought there is no such thing as a healthy fried food, this book will change your mind.

You don't need a cluttered kitchen with so many fancy cookware. You don't need any special culinary skills. Air frying requires little effort, making it one of the hottest food trends for the coming year!

3. An easy press-and-go operation will save you a tone of time.

With this revolutionary "fix-it and forget-it" system, air-fried meals practically cook themselves. Busy moms will be delighted! They require just a little prep and voilà – dinner is ready in minutes! From here on out, you can cook an entire meal using a super-heated air. There is the Air Fryer divider that allows you to cook two different types of food; just make sure to follow the cooking chart. It is fast, convenient, and easy to use. Fish fillets, chicken nuggets, French fries, cakes and other "greasy" foods are back on the menu! Moreover, you will end up with only one cooking basket for cleaning. The Air Fryer keeps your kitchen clean and pleasant; there is no smell and no mess!

4. An effective weight loss trick.

If you are searching for a cooking method that can help you get a flat tummy, an Air Fryer may become your first choice. If you tend to boost flavors and cut calories, you just need to select the right cooking technique. Thanks to the Air Fryer, you will enjoy your favorite fried food and lose weight at the same time. You don't have to avoid saucy steaks, luscious cheesecakes, and French fries. You just need a kitchen device that can help you make the most of your food. This incredible machine allows you to enjoy nourishing, great-tasting and well-balanced meals without excess calories.

Simply put, a controlled cooking time and a super-heated environment are key factors to a healthier cooking and more successful dieting. A hot air is a new oil; you should cut fat and calories not flavor! All these benefits make an Air Fryer the right option when it comes to healthy and enjoyable eating.

A Word about Our Recipe Collection

This recipe collection contains 135 simple yet tasty recipes that are divided into 10 categories. In addition to the surprising variety of great ketogenic recipe, this cookbook is chockfull of cooking secrets, serving ideas, tips and tricks for better air frying.

You will find timeless recipes, from quick and easy vegan meals to slurp-worthy stews and elegant dessert. All the recipes are written in an easy-to-follow way that will guide you every step of the way in order to prepare the best keto meals ever. The recipes are accompanied by nutritional information so you will be able to track your nutrition and count carbs. This recipe collection is designed to help you create homemade restaurant-quality meals easily and effortlessly even on those busy weeknights.

If you are tired of dieting, experimenting with too many weight-management strategies, the Air Fryer will transform your life. You will be surprised what this innovative device can do in the kitchen. Get started with the best ketogenic Air Fryer recipes that follow. Enjoy!

POULTRY

1. Za'atar Chicken Fillets with Chili Mayo

(Ready in about 35 minutes | Servings 4)

INGREDIENTS

For the Chicken Fillets:

3 teaspoons pork rinds

1 ½ teaspoons Za'atar seasonings

1 pound chicken fillets

1 yellow onion, sliced

2 garlic cloves, smashed

1 ¼ cups chicken broth, preferably
   homemade

2 sprigs rosemary, leaves picked

For the Homemade Chili Mayo:

1/2 cup mayonnaise

2 tablespoons sour cream

1 teaspoon stone ground mustard

1 tablespoon chipotle chili sauce

DIRECTIONS

- In a shallow bowl, mix the pork rinds with the Za'atar seasonings. Toss the chicken with this mixture until it is well coated.
- Preheat your Air Fryer to 360 degrees F. Spritz the baking dish with a nonstick cooking spray or brush with 1 teaspoon of olive oil.
- Arrange the seasoned chicken fillets in a baking dish.
- Cook for 25 minutes, flipping the chicken fillets once. Lower the temperature on the Air Fryer to 340 degrees F.
- Add the remaining ingredients for the chicken fillets. Cook an additional 8 minutes.
- Meanwhile, make the homemade chili mayo by whisking the mayonnaise, sour cream, mustard and chili sauce. Serve with warm chicken fillets.

Per serving: 422 Calories; 23.2g Fat; 6.6g Carbs; 43.8g Protein;

2. Sunday Cheesy Turkey Fillets

(Ready in about 50 minutes | Servings 4)

INGREDIENTS

Nonstick cooking spray
1/4 cup Romano cheese, freshly grated
1/4 cup cornflakes
1 ½ tablespoons olive oil

1 pound turkey fillets, sliced into 4 pieces
1/4 cup Colby cheese, shredded

DIRECTIONS

- Preheat your Air Fryer to 350 degrees F for a couple of minutes. Spritz the cooking basket with a nonstick cooking spray.
- Combine the Romano cheese and cornflakes in a shallow dish. Brush the turkey with olive oil.
- Now, dip each piece of turkey into the cheese/cornflakes mixture. Cook in the preheated Air Fryer for 20 minutes.
- Flip the turkey fillets and cook on the other side for 15 minutes longer. The internal temperature should reach 165 degrees F.
- Lastly, top with the shredded Colby cheese and cook 3 to 4 minutes more or until the cheese has melted.
- Let the turkey fillets rest for 6 to 7 minutes before serving. Bon appétit!

Per serving: 681 Calories; 60.1g Fat; 5.9g Carbs; 26g Protein;

3. Mexican-Style Turkey Delight

(Ready in about 30 minutes | Servings 6)

INGREDIENTS

1 teaspoon olive oil
1 ½ pounds turkey breasts, cubed
1 egg, beaten
1/3 cup pork rinds
1 tablespoon olive oil
1 bell pepper, deveined and sliced

1 chili pepper, chopped
1 cup cauliflower florets
1/2 cup leek, sliced
2 garlic cloves, minced
1/4 cup dry white wine
1 tablespoon soy sauce

DIRECTIONS

- Preheat your Air Fryer to 390 degrees F. Brush a cooking basket with 1 teaspoon of olive oil.
- Then, coat the cubed turkey breasts with the beaten egg, and lastly, dip into the crushed pork rinds.
- Cook the turkey breasts at 390 degrees F for 20 minutes.
- Meanwhile, preheat a sauté pan over a moderately high heat. Heat 1 tablespoon of olive oil until sizzling.
- Now, sauté the vegetables, gradually adding the dry white wine, until they are tender to your liking. Heat off. Add the soy sauce and stir to combine.
- Add the air-fried turkey and stir until everything is well incorporated. Serve immediately with mustard and horseradish mayo.

Per serving: 313 Calories; 18.7g Fat; 4.6g Carbs; 30.2g Protein;

4. Classic Shiritaki Noodles with Meat Sauce

(Ready in about 30 minutes | Servings 4)

INGREDIENTS

1/2 leek, chopped

2 garlic cloves, minced

1/2 pound turkey, ground

1/2 pound chicken, ground

1/2 teaspoon flaky sea salt

1/4 teaspoon ground black pepper

1/2 teaspoon smoked cayenne pepper

1 teaspoon dried oregano

1/2 teaspoon dried rosemary

1/2 teaspoon dried basil

2 ripe tomatoes, crushed

1 (7-ounce) shiritaki noodles

DIRECTIONS

- Start by preheating your Air Fryer to 380 degrees F.
- Add the leek, garlic, turkey, and chicken to your Air Fryer. Cook for 10 minutes.
- Add the salt, black pepper, cayenne pepper, oregano, rosemary, basil, and tomatoes. Cook an additional 15 minutes.
- In a large, deep pan, bring a lightly-salted water to a rolling boil. Boil the noodles, stirring periodically to keep the pasta from sticking to the bottom of your pan.
- Once cooked, drain the noodles well. Serve with hot Bolognese sauce. Bon appétit!

Per serving: 200 Calories; 10.8g Fat; 5.9g Carbs; 19.9g Protein;

5. Chinese-Style Parmesan Crusted Chicken

(Ready in about 35 minutes | Servings 6)

INGREDIENTS

1 teaspoon sesame oil

2 tablespoons lime juice

1/4 cup Chinese cooking wine

2 tablespoons tamari sauce

2 tablespoons pureed tomato

1 tablespoon sambal oelek

2 cloves garlic, minced

6 chicken drumsticks

3/4 cup almond flour

1 teaspoon salt

1/2 teaspoon smoked cayenne pepper

1/2 teaspoon black peppercorns, freshly cracked

2 eggs

1 ¼ cups parmesan cheese, grated

1 teaspoon Five-spice powder

DIRECTIONS

- In a mixing bowl, thoroughly whisk 1 teaspoon of the sesame oil, lime juice, wine, tamari sauce, tomato, sambal oelek and garlic.
- Add the chicken drumsticks to the marinade and let them sit for 2 hours in the refrigerator.
- Add the almond flour, salt, smoked cayenne pepper and black peppercorns to the shallow plate and combine well.
- Whisk the eggs in a separate shallow bowl. Then, mix the grated parmesan cheese and Five-spice powder in a third shallow bowl.
- Dip each drumstick into the almond flour mixture, then, dip into the eggs and lastly, coat with the parmesan mixture on all sides.
- Preheat your Air Fryer to 380 degrees F.
- Air-fry the chicken drumsticks for 25 minutes, flipping them over halfway through. Serve right away!

Per serving: 356 Calories; 21.8g Fat; 5.4g Carbs; 32.8g Protein;

6. Juicy Marinated Chicken Legs

(Ready in about 45 minutes + marinating time | Servings 6)

INGREDIENTS

1 ½ tablespoons olive oil
1 teaspoon paprika
1 teaspoon ground cumin
1 teaspoon sea salt
1/2 teaspoon ground black pepper
1/2 teaspoon ground bay leaf

2 garlic cloves, minced
1 cup dry red wine
1 tablespoon Worcestershire sauce
1 teaspoon fresh ginger, grated
1 ½ pounds chicken legs

DIRECTIONS

- Combine the olive oil, paprika, cumin, sea salt, black pepper, ground bay leaf, garlic, wine, Worcestershire sauce, and ginger in a saucepan.
- Bring the mixture to a rolling boil for 1 to 2 minutes; then, reduce heat and simmer for a further 10 minutes, stirring periodically.
- Allow the marinade to cool; now, marinate the chicken legs. Next, pat them dry.
- Brush the sides and bottom of a cooking basket with oil.
- Cook the marinated chicken legs at 380 degrees for 35 minutes, flipping them over half-way through. Serve with salad of your choice.

Per serving: 278 Calories; 12.1g Fat; 2.3g Carbs; 33.1g Protein;

7. Turkey Burgers with Mustard Sauce

(Ready in about 15 minutes | Servings 6)

INGREDIENTS

1 ½ pounds ground turkey

1/4 teaspoon ground marjoram

A pinch of grated nutmeg

1/2 teaspoon cayenne pepper

1 teaspoon flaky sea salt

1/4 teaspoon black pepper, preferably
  freshly ground

For the Mustard Sauce:

2 tablespoons erythritol

2 tablespoons sour cream

1/4 cup mayonnaise

2 tablespoons Dijon mustard

DIRECTIONS

- Begin by preheating your Air Fryer to 330 degrees F. Thoroughly combine the ground turkey with the marjoram, nutmeg, cayenne pepper, salt and ground black pepper.
- Shape the mixture into 6 burgers.
- Spritz a cooking basket with a nonstick cooking spray. Cook the burgers for 8 to 12 minutes or to the desired degree of doneness.
- Meanwhile, whisk all of the ingredients for the mustard sauce. Serve the warm burgers with the prepared sauce and burger buns. Bon appétit!

Per serving: 209 Calories; 12.4g Fat; 0.8g Carbs; 23.2g Protein;

8. Fried Teriyaki Turkey Strips

(Ready in about 15 minutes + marinating time | Servings 8)

INGREDIENTS

2 tablespoons soy sauce

2 tablespoons apple cider vinegar

1/4 cup erythritol

1 tablespoon olive oil

1 onion, chopped

2 cloves garlic, smashed

1/2 teaspoon salt

1/2 teaspoon cayenne pepper

2 pounds turkey breasts, cut into strips

2 egg whites, beaten

1 cup parmesan cheese, grated

DIRECTIONS

- In a mixing dish, thoroughly combine the soy sauce, apple cider vinegar, erythritol, olive oil, onion, garlic, salt, and cayenne pepper. Add turkey and let it marinate for 1-2 hours.
- Pat the turkey strips dry and dip them into the egg whites, and finally, dip into the parmesan cheese.
- Brush the Air Fryer cooking basket with olive oil.
- Cook at 360 degrees for about 12 minutes or until thoroughly cooked. Serve immediately.

Per serving: 269 Calories; 13.9g Fat; 4.2g Carbs; 29.7g Protein;

9. Chicken Sausages with Sriracha Mayo

(Ready in about 15 minutes | Servings 4)

INGREDIENTS

4 Italian chicken sausages

For the Sauce:
1/2 cup keto mayonnaise
1 garlic clove, minced
2 tablespoons Sriracha
1/4 teaspoon salt

DIRECTIONS

- Begin by preheating your Air Fryer to 360 degrees F. Prick holes in the sausages.
- Place the sausages in the cooking basket. Cook about 6 to 7 minutes.
- Turn the sausages and cook another 6 to 7 minutes or until they're thoroughly cooked.
- Meanwhile, make the sauce by whisking the mayonnaise, garlic, Sriracha, and salt. Serve the warm sausages over the dinner rolls. Bon appétit!

Per serving: 277 Calories; 25.4g Fat; 3.1g Carbs; 8.7g Protein;

10. Queso Añejo Chicken Ole

(Ready in about 30 minutes | Servings 6)

INGREDIENTS

2 tablespoons sesame oil
Salt and ground black pepper, to taste
10 ounces salsa
1 ½ pounds chicken breasts
1 cup Queso Añejo, shredded

DIRECTIONS

- Begin by preheating your Air Fryer to 380 degrees F.
- To make the sauce, mix the sesame oil, salt, black pepper, and salsa in a bowl.
- Arrange the chicken in a baking dish. Pour the sauce over them.
- Cook for 15 minutes, turning halfway through. Afterwards, top the chicken with the shredded cheese and bake an additional 10 minutes. Bon appétit!

Per serving: 322 Calories; 16.3g Fat; 3g Carbs; 38.9g Protein;

11. Taco Chicken Drumsticks with Vegetables

(Ready in about 40 minutes | Servings 6)

INGREDIENTS

1 ½ pounds chicken drumsticks

1 tablespoon Taco seasoning mix

2 carrots, cut into matchsticks

1 green bell pepper, sliced

1 red bell pepper, sliced

1 yellow onion, clicked

1 teaspoon sea salt

1/2 teaspoon ground black pepper

1/2 teaspoon red pepper flakes, crushed

1 tablespoon olive oil

DIRECTIONS

- Start by preheating your Air Fryer to 370 degrees F.
- Coat the cooking basket of your Air Fryer with a piece of aluminum foil. Add the chicken drumsticks and sprinkle them with the Taco seasoning mix.
- Cook for 20 minutes, flipping them halfway through. Then, reserve the chicken drumsticks, keeping them warm.
- Toss the vegetables with salt, black pepper, and red pepper; drizzle them with olive oil and set your Air Fryer to cook at 380 degrees F.
- Cook the vegetables for 15 minutes. Add the prepared chicken back to the Air Fryer and cook an additional 5 minutes.
- Transfer the chicken and vegetables to a serving platter and eat warm. Bon appétit!

Per serving: 280 Calories; 10.1g Fat; 7.2g Carbs; 37.6g Protein;

12. Family Cheesy Chicken Casserole

(Ready in about 20 minutes | Servings 4)

INGREDIENTS

1 pound chicken breasts, cut into strips

1 teaspoon ground cumin

1 teaspoon chipotle powder

1/2 teaspoon garlic powder

1 teaspoon shallot powder

1 teaspoon porcini powder

1/2 teaspoon flaky sea salt

1 teaspoon mixed whole peppercorns

1/2 cup Romano cheese, grated

1 cup ripe tomatoes, chopped

1 bell pepper, deveined and sliced

1 yellow onion, sliced

10 ounces Colby cheese, shredded

2 tablespoons fresh parsley, chopped

DIRECTIONS

- Preheat your Air Fryer to 360 degrees F.
- Toss the chicken with the ground cumin, chipotle powder, garlic powder, shallot powder, porcini powder, and flaky sea salt.
- Coat the cooking basket with a piece of foil. Place the chicken in the cooking basket; add the mixed peppercorns and Romano cheese.
- Add the tomatoes, bell pepper, and onion. Top with the shredded Colby cheese. Bake for 12 minutes or until thoroughly cooked.
- Sprinkle fresh parsley on top and serve warm. Bon appétit!

Per serving: 556 Calories; 38.5g Fat; 6.2g Carbs; 45.5g Protein;

13. Thanksgiving Bacon Wrapped Meatloaf

(Ready in about 35 minutes | Servings 4)

INGREDIENTS

1 pound ground turkey

1 egg, beaten

1/4 cup saltine crackers, crushed

1 cup yellow onions, chopped

2 garlic cloves, finely minced

1 teaspoon Dijon mustard

1/4 teaspoon hot red pepper sauce

1/3 cup minced parsley

1 teaspoon dried rosemary

1/2 teaspoon dried oregano

1 teaspoon dried basil

Sea salt and ground black pepper, to
   taste

4 ounces bacon, thin-sliced

DIRECTIONS

- Begin by preheating your Air Fryer to 380 degrees F. Line a cooking basket with a sheet of foil.
- Thoroughly combine the ground turkey, egg, saltine crackers, yellow onions, garlic, mustard, hot red pepper sauce, and minced parsley. Season with rosemary, oregano, basil, salt, and ground black pepper.
- Shape the mixture into a loaf with wet hands and place in the cooking basket. Brush the meatloaf with oil. Now, place the slices of bacon crosswise over the loaf. Make sure to overlap them slightly.
- Bake for 30 minutes or until a meat thermometer registers 160 degrees F.
- Allow the meatloaf to stand for a couple of minutes before slicing. Serve warm with mashed potatoes.

Per serving: 416 Calories; 25.7g Fat; 5.7g Carbs; 43.6g Protein;

14. Turkey Bacon with Broccoli

(Ready in about 20 minutes | Servings 6)

INGREDIENTS

1 pound turkey bacon, sliced

1 pound broccoli, broken into florets

2 garlic cloves, minced

1/2 teaspoon flaky sea salt

1/3 teaspoon ground black pepper

1/3 teaspoon red pepper flakes

1/4 teaspoon dried dill weed

1 tablespoon olive oil

DIRECTIONS

- Begin by preheating your Air Fryer to 390 degrees F.
- Place the slices of bacon in the pan and insert it into your Air Fryer. Cook for 8 minutes. Reserve.
- Toss the broccoli with garlic, sea salt, black pepper, red pepper, and dill; drizzle with olive oil. Now, preheat your Air Fryer to 400 degrees F.
- Cook for 8 minutes. Serve the cooked bacon with the broccoli. Bon appétit!

Per serving: 403 Calories; 36.2g Fat; 2.6g Carbs; 16.8g Protein;

PORK

15. Easy Pork Cutlets with Enchilada Sauce

(Ready in about 25 minutes | Servings 4)

INGREDIENTS

4 pork cutlets
1 egg white
Salt and ground black pepper, to taste
1 teaspoon red pepper flakes, crushed
1/2 cup Parmesan cheese, grated
1/2 cup pork rinds

For Enchilada Sauce:
1 tablespoon olive oil
1 tablespoon flaxseed meal
1 large-sized tomato, chopped
1/2 teaspoon erythritol
1/2 teaspoon chili powder
1/2 teaspoon garlic powder
1/2 teaspoon shallot powder
Kosher salt and freshly ground black
   pepper, to taste

DIRECTIONS

- Preheat your Air Fryer to 380 degrees F.
- In a mixing bowl, whisk the egg white together with the salt, black pepper, and red pepper flakes.
- Dip the pork cutlets in the egg mixture. Then, coat the pork cutlets with the parmesan and pork rinds. Cook for 15 minutes.
- Meanwhile, heat the olive oil in a pan that is preheated over moderate heat. Gradually add the flaxseed meal and stir to combine for 2 minutes.
- Add the remaining ingredients for the sauce, bringing it to a boil; then, turn the heat to a medium-low; simmer an additional 8 minutes.
- Serve over the pork cutlets. Enjoy!

Per serving: 496 Calories; 27.8g Fat; 5.5g Carbs; 53.4g Protein;

16. Festive Roasted Pork Belly

(Ready in about 2 hours | Servings 6)

INGREDIENTS

1 ½ pounds pork belly

1 ½ tablespoons oyster sauce

1 teaspoon stone grain mustard

1/2 teaspoon hot red pepper sauce

2 tablespoons tamari sauce

2 tablespoons Shaoxing rice wine

1 tablespoon olive oil

1 tablespoon raw honey

1/2 teaspoon dried thyme

1/2 teaspoon dried oregano

1/2 teaspoon flaky sea salt

1/2 teaspoon ground black pepper

DIRECTIONS

- Blanch the pork belly in a large pot of boiling water approximately 15 minutes. Now, prick the skin with a steel skewer.
- Place the pork in a mixing bowl. Add the remaining ingredients and toss to coat on all sides. Place the pork in your refrigerator and let it stand for at least 1 hour.
- Then, preheat your Air Fryer to 380 degrees F. Cook the marinated pork for 12 minutes.
- Turn the temperature to 330 degrees and cook for another 25 minutes, basting with the remaining marinade.
- Serve warm with baked potatoes. Bon appétit!

Per serving: 623 Calories; 62.4g Fat; 3.8g Carbs; 10.8g Protein;

17. Tortilla Chip-Crusted Pork

(Ready in about 20 minutes | Servings 8)

INGREDIENTS

2 pounds pork shoulder, sliced 3/4-
   inch thick
1 teaspoon salt
1/4 teaspoon ground black pepper
2 eggs, whisked

1 cup Parmesan cheese, grated
1/4 teaspoon cayenne pepper
1 teaspoon garlic powder
1/2 teaspoon chipotle powder

DIRECTIONS

- Begin by preheating your Air Fryer to 390 degrees F; now, spritz the cooking basket with a nonstick spray.
- Sprinkle each piece of the pork with salt and black pepper. Add the eggs in a shallow bowl.
- Combine the crushed tortilla chips, cayenne pepper, garlic powder, and chipotle powder in another shallow bowl.
- Dip each piece of pork in the eggs and then in the tortilla chips mixture.
- Cook for 15 minutes, flipping once or twice; work in batches to ensure even cooking.

Per serving: 388 Calories; 25.9g Fat; 2.1g Carbs; 34.2g Protein;

18. Herbed Pork Sausage Meatballs

(Ready in about 20 minutes | Servings 4)

INGREDIENTS

3/4 pound pork sausage (bangers)
1/4 pound ground beef
1 leek, finely chopped
2 garlic cloves, finely minced
1 teaspoon dried thyme

1 teaspoon dried rosemary
1/2 teaspoon dried oregano
1 ½ teaspoons whole grain mustard
Salt and ground black pepper, to taste

DIRECTIONS

- Preheat your Air Fryer to 380 degrees F.
- Cut the sausage and squeeze out the sausage meat. Add to a large-sized bowl. Add the other ingredients and mix to combine well.
- Shape the sausage mixture into meatballs with damp hands.
- Cook for 13 to 16 minutes, shaking occasionally. Serve over warm polenta and enjoy!

Per serving: 179 Calories; 7.8g Fat; 4.8g Carbs; 22.4g Protein;

19. BBQ Pork Ribs

(Ready in about 30 minutes | Servings 4)

INGREDIENTS

1 pound pork ribs, cut into 2 sections
2 garlic cloves, halved
1/2 teaspoon salt
1/4 teaspoon red pepper flakes,
   crushed

Freshly ground black pepper, to your
   liking
1/2 teaspoon liquid smoke

DIRECTIONS

- Blanch the pork ribs in a pot of a lightly-salted boiling water. Drain the pork ribs and dry them with kitchen towels.
- Rub the pork ribs with the garlic halves. Season with salt, red pepper flakes, and ground black pepper.
- Lastly, drizzle with liquid smoke.
- Cook in the preheated Air Fryer at 380 degrees F for 25 minutes. Bon appétit!

Per serving: 161 Calories; 6.4g Fat; 0.5g Carbs; 23.6g Protein;

20. Roast Pork Tenderloin with Chimichurri Sauce

(Ready in about 40 minutes | Servings 6)

INGREDIENTS

1 ½ pounds pork tenderloin
1 ½ tablespoons butter, at room temperature
1/4 teaspoon ground black pepper
Flaky sea salt, to taste

For Chimichurri Sauce:
2 tablespoons fresh parsley, chopped
2 garlic cloves, very finely chopped
1 onion, chopped
3 tablespoons extra-virgin olive oil
1/2 teaspoon dried crushed red pepper
1 ½ tablespoons wine vinegar

DIRECTIONS

- Start by preheating your Air Fryer to 370 degrees F. Rub the pork tenderloins with the softened butter; season with black pepper and sea salt.
- Cook for 25 minutes. Decrease the temperature to 360 degrees F, flip the pork tenderloins and cook on the other side for 12 minutes more.
- Meanwhile, whisk all ingredients for the sauce. Serve with the warm pork tenderloin. Bon appétit!

Per serving: 224 Calories; 9.8g Fat; 2.5g Carbs; 30g Protein;

21. Pork and Pancetta Meatloaf

(Ready in about 35 minutes | Servings 6)

INGREDIENTS

For the Meatloaf:
1 pound ground pork
1/4 pounds pancetta, chopped
2 teaspoons Provençal herbs
1 egg, beaten
1/2 cup pork rind
1 cup white onion, chopped
2 garlic cloves, minced
Kosher salt and freshly ground pepper,
   to taste
1 teaspoon smoked paprika
1/4 teaspoon dried oregano
1 teaspoon dried sage, crushed

For the Sauce:
1 cup tomato sauce, canned, no salt
   added
1 teaspoon erythritol
1/2 teaspoon ground black pepper
1/4 teaspoon mustard powder
1/8 teaspoon grated nutmeg

DIRECTIONS

- Start by preheating your Air Fryer to 390 degrees F.
- Combine all ingredients for the meatloaf in a mixing dish. Transfer to a baking pan and shape into a loaf.
- Mix all ingredients for the sauce. Pour the sauce over the meatloaf. Put the baking pan into the Air Fryer cooking basket. Bake 30 minutes in the preheated Air Fryer.
- Allow your meatloaf to cool slightly before serving. Enjoy!

Per serving: 323 Calories; 20.1g Fat; 4.7g Carbs; 29.3g Protein;

22. Bubble & Squeak with Ham and Feta

(Ready in about 35 minutes | Servings 3)

INGREDIENTS

4 eggs

6 slices of ham, chopped

1 cup Brussels sprouts, chopped

1/2 yellow onion, chopped

1/2 cup feta cheese, crumbled

1 teaspoon dried basil

1/2 teaspoon dried dill weed

1/2 teaspoon sea salt

1/4 teaspoon black pepper, preferably
   freshly ground

DIRECTIONS

- Whisk the eggs in a medium-sized mixing dish. Add the chopped ham, Brussels sprouts, and onions.
- Stir in the cheese; stir to combine well. Season with dried basil, dill, salt and black pepper; spoon the mixture into a baking pan.
- Place in the cooking basket of your Air Fryer.
- Bake for 30 minutes at 360 degrees F. Serve warm and enjoy!

Per serving: 317 Calories; 21.3g Fat; 6.5g Carbs; 24.4g Protein;

23. Fried Bacon with Rutabaga Fries

(Ready in about 1 hour | Servings 4)

INGREDIENTS

8 rashes pork bacon

1 pound rutabaga, peeled and cut sticks

2 teaspoons olive oil

Flaky sea salt and black pepper, to taste

1/2 teaspoon cayenne pepper

1 teaspoon rosemary

1 teaspoon marjoram

1 teaspoon basil

1 teaspoon garlic powder

DIRECTIONS

- Preheat your Air Fryer to 400 degrees F. Arrange the rashes of pork bacon in the cooking basket.
- Now, cook the bacon for 8 minutes or to your desired doneness; reserve.
- Meanwhile, place the rutabaga in a bowl of cold water and let them soak for 35 minutes. Pat them dry with a kitchen towel.
- Toss the rutabaga with olive oil, salt, black pepper, cayenne pepper, rosemary, marjoram, basil, and garlic powder until they are well coated.
- Cook the seasoned rutabaga for 18 minutes at 400 degrees F. Check for doneness and top with the reserved bacon.
- Cook for 1 minute more at 370 degrees F or until thoroughly cooked. Bon appétit!

Per serving: 344 Calories; 29.6g Fat; 6.1g Carbs; 9.9g Protein;

24. Easy Pork Chops with Onion

(Ready in about 20 minutes | Servings 5)

INGREDIENTS

5 bone-in pork chops, trimmed of fat

2 garlic cloves, halved

2 tablespoons whole grain mustard

Se salt and ground black pepper, to
    taste

1 teaspoon paprika

1 onion, cut into 5 thick slices

DIRECTIONS

- Start by preheating your Air Fryer to 400 degrees F.
- Rub the pork chops with the garlic halves and mustard on both sides. Sprinkle with salt, black pepper, and paprika.
- Arrange the pork chops in the cooking basket. Cook for 5 minutes. Then, turn over and cook another 4 minutes.
- Place a slice of onion on each pork chop and continue to cook an additional 4 minutes. Serve warm with refreshing cucumber and yogurt salad. Bon appétit!

Per serving: 273 Calories; 9.1g Fat; 2.5g Carbs; 42.7g Protein;

25. Boston Butt with Sherry Wine Sauce

(Ready in about 1 hour 10 minutes | Servings 8)

INGREDIENTS

2 pounds Boston butt

1 ½ tablespoons olive oil

1/2 cup onions, minced

1 teaspoon salt

1/2 teaspoon ground black pepper

1 teaspoon dried Mexican oregano

2 garlic cloves, minced

2 tablespoons fresh coriander, chopped

1 teaspoon chili pepper, minced

1/2 cup dry white wine

DIRECTIONS

- Make shallow cuts on the meat by using a sharp knife. Add the remaining ingredients and marinate the meat overnight.
- Preheat your Air Fryer to 350 degrees F for 5 to 10 minutes. Cook the marinated Boston butt for 55 minutes, turning halfway through the cooking time.
- In the meantime, make the sauce. Cook the marinade in a pan over medium-high until reduced by half.
- Slice the prepared Boston butt and serve with the sauce on the side. Bon appétit!

Per serving: 352 Calories; 24.1g Fat; 1.7g Carbs; 30.1g Protein;

26. The Best Pork Sliders Ever

(Ready in about 25 minutes | Servings 6)

INGREDIENTS

1 ½ pounds ground pork
1 teaspoon Swiss vegetable bouillon
    powder
2 teaspoon Shoyu sauce
2 green onions, chopped
1 teaspoon garlic paste
1 teaspoon shallot powder
1 teaspoon chipotle powder
Salt and ground black pepper, to taste
1 ½ teaspoons dried parsley flakes
6 slices Cheddar cheese

For the slider buns:
1/4 cup mozzarella cheese, grated
3 ounces cream cheese
2 eggs
1 3/4 cup almond flour
1 teaspoon baking powder

DIRECTIONS

- Mix the ground pork, bouillon powder, Shoyu sauce, green onions, garlic paste, shallot powder, chipotle powder, salt, ground black pepper, and parsley in a large bowl.
- Shape the meat mixture into 6 patties with oiled hands; transfer to a cooking basket.
- Cook in the preheated your Air Fryer at 390 degrees F for 20 minutes; work in batches.
- To make the keto slider buns, mix the dry ingredients for the buns; then, mix the wet ingredients. Add the wet mixture to the dry mixture; mix to combine well.
- Preheat your oven to 400 degrees F; place a rack in the middle of the oven. Line a baking sheet with parchment paper. Bake your buns for 12 minutes or until the outside has browned.
- Place one slice of cheese on each patty and serve with the slider buns.

Per serving: 480 Calories; 33g Fat; 6g Carbs; 38.1g Protein;

27. Garam Masala and Orange Pork

(Ready in about 3 hours 30 minutes | Servings 6)

INGREDIENTS

1 ½ pounds baby back ribs

Sea salt and ground black pepper, to taste

1 teaspoon fresh ginger root, minced

1 teaspoon garam masala spice

1/2 cup fresh orange juice

1/4 cup soy sauce

1 tablespoon olive oil

1/4 cup fresh cilantro, chopped

DIRECTIONS

- Discard the membranes from the back of the pork ribs; cut the pork ribs into 3 to 4 pieces.
- Toss the baby back ribs with salt, pepper, ginger, garam masala, orange juice, soy sauce, and olive oil. Transfer to the refrigerator and let it marinate for 3 hours.
- Preheat your Air Fryer to 360 degrees F. Discard the marinade and place the pork ribs in the cooking basket. Cook for 13 minutes.
- Turn and cook for 16 minutes on the other side.
- Meanwhile, cook the marinade in a saucepan over a moderate flame; cook until the sauce is reduced by half and slightly thickened.
- Pour the sauce over the pork ribs, garnish with fresh cilantro and serve warm.

Per serving: 288 Calories; 16.2g Fat; 3g Carbs; 30.7g Protein;

28. Spicy Habanero Pork Filet Mignon

(Ready in about 3 hours 20 minutes | Servings 4)

INGREDIENTS

4 (4-ounce) pork fillets

2 garlic cloves, pressed

1/2 white onion, chopped

1 teaspoon Dijon mustard

1 teaspoon fresh ginger root, grated

1 bell pepper, chopped

1 Habanero pepper, chopped

Salt and black pepper, to taste

2 tablespoons soy sauce

2 tablespoons champagne vinegar

1 ½ tablespoons sesame oil

DIRECTIONS

- Place the pork filets in a re-sealable zipper storage bag. Add the remaining ingredients and shake vigorously to combine.
- Place in the refrigerator and allow it to marinate for 3 hours.
- Preheat your Air Fryer to 380 degrees F. Cook for 15 minutes, flipping once. Serve with mashed potatoes and beet root salad.

Per serving: 420 Calories; 24.2g Fat; 5.9g Carbs; 42.7g Protein;

BEEF

29. Bologna Sausage with Mushrooms and Peppers

(Ready in about 25 minutes | Servings 4)

INGREDIENTS

6 ounces Bologna sausages

1 ½ tablespoons Dijon mustard

1 tablespoon olive oil

1 cup button mushrooms, sliced

1/2 white onion, chopped

1 red bell pepper, sliced

1 green bell pepper, sliced

1/2 teaspoon garlic powder

1/2 teaspoon cayenne pepper

Salt and black pepper, to taste

DIRECTIONS

- Preheat your Air Fryer to 380 degrees for about 4 minutes.
- Cook the sausages for 7 minutes; turn them over and cook an additional 7 minutes; top with mustard and reserve.
- Meanwhile, heat the oil in a sauté pan that is preheated over a moderately high heat. Sauté the mushrooms with the onions and bell peppers.
- Season with garlic powder, cayenne powder, salt, and black pepper and stir to combine. Transfer to a serving platter along with the reserved sausages.
- Serve with dinner rolls. Bon appétit!

Per serving: 310 Calories; 26.4g Fat; 6.4g Carbs; 12g Protein;

30. Ranchero and Scallion Burgers

(Ready in about 35 minutes | Servings 4)

INGREDIENTS

1 1/3 pounds ground chuck
2 garlic cloves, minced
1 jalapeño pepper, finely minced
1/2 cup scallions, peeled and chopped
Salt and ground black pepper, to taste
1 tablespoon tomato puree
1/4 cup Parmesan cheese, grated
1/2 cup iceberg lettuce, shredded
1/2 cup chunky salsa

For the keto rolls:
1 cup almond flour
1/4 cup coconut flour
1/3 cup psyllium husks
1/4 packed cup flax seed meal
1 teaspoon cream of tartar
1/2 teaspoon baking soda
1 teaspoon garlic powder
A pinch of salt
1 tablespoon caraway seeds
4 eggs
1 cup water, lukewarm

DIRECTIONS

- Preheat your Air Fryer to 390 degrees F.
- In a mixing bowl, thoroughly combine the ground chuck with the garlic, jalapeño pepper, scallions, salt, black pepper, tomato puree, and cheese.
- Form this meat mixture into 4 patties. Bake for 25 minutes.
- To make the keto rolls, in a mixing bowl, thoroughly combine the flour, psyllium husks, flax seed meal. Add the cream of tartar and baking soda.
- Now, stir in the garlic powder, salt, and caraway seeds.
- Now, fold in the eggs and mix to combine. Gradually pour in the water and mix again. Make the buns using a spoon; place them on a baking sheet that is lined with a parchment paper.
- Bake in the preheated oven at 350 degrees F for about 45 minutes.
- Serve the prepared patties over the keto rolls, garnished with iceberg lettuce and chunky salsa. Bon appétit!

Per serving: 405 Calories; 23.8g Fat; 6.9g Carbs; 40.1g Protein;

31. Mint and Cilantro Chuck

(Ready in about 20 minutes + marinating time | Servings 4)

INGREDIENTS

1 ¼ pounds chuck, cut into four portions

1 teaspoon salt

1/2 teaspoon ground black pepper

1/2 teaspoon cayenne pepper

1/4 cup fresh cilantro, finely chopped

1/4 cup mint, finely minced

4 garlic cloves, finely minced

1 teaspoon cayenne pepper

1 teaspoon ground cumin

2 tablespoons olive oil

3 tablespoons champagne vinegar

DIRECTIONS

- In a mixing dish, combine the chuck with the other ingredients; wrap with foil. Transfer the dish to your refrigerator; let it marinate at least 2 hours,
- Preheat your Air Fryer to 400 degrees F for 5 minutes
- Discard the marinade and place the chuck on a double layer rack in your Air Fryer. Cook for 12 minutes, flipping once. Bon appétit!

Per serving: 436 Calories; 34.4g Fat; 1.6g Carbs; 28.6g Protein;

32. Flank Steak with Roasted Garlic Sauce

(Ready in about 40 minutes + marinating time | Servings 5)

INGREDIENTS

1 ½ pounds flank steak

2 tablespoons sesame oil

1/4 cup soy sauce

2 tablespoons xylitol

2 tablespoons red wine vinegar

1 tablespoon fresh chives, chopped

1 teaspoon basil

1 teaspoon oregano

1/2 teaspoon hot pepper sauce

Salt and freshly ground black pepper, to taste

1 garlic bulb, peeled

For the Sauce:

2 tablespoons butter

1/2 cup whipping cream

1 ½ tablespoons flaxseed meal

1/2 cup Parmesan cheese, shredded

DIRECTIONS

- Start by preheating the Air Fryer to 390 degrees F for 5 to 10 minutes. Spritz a cooking basket with a nonstick cooking spray and roast the garlic for 10 minutes; reserve.
- In a mixing dish, combine the flank steak with the sesame oil, soy sauce, xylitol, vinegar, chives, basil, oregano, hot pepper sauce, salt, and black pepper.
- Transfer the dish to your refrigerator and marinate it for at least 3 hours and up to overnight.
- Now, preheat the Air Fryer to 400 degrees F. Roast the flank steak for 12 minutes.
- Squeeze the pulp from the garlic cloves. Cook the garlic, butter, whipping cream, and flaxseed meal in a pan over medium-high heat, stirring frequently.
- Cook until the sauce is thickened. Heat off; stir in the Parmesan cheese. Serve with the prepared flank steak.

Per serving: 390 Calories; 24.6g Fat; 6.8g Carbs; 33.8g Protein;

33. Delicious Beef Meatballs

(Ready in about 20 minutes | Servings 4)

INGREDIENTS

1 ½ pounds beef, ground

1 teaspoon Worcestershire sauce

Flaky sea salt and freshly ground black
    pepper, to taste

1 teaspoon paprika

1/2 teaspoon granulated garlic

2 tablespoons scallions, chopped

4 tablespoons ketchup

4 teaspoons mustard

1/2 red onion, chopped

DIRECTIONS

- In a mixing dish, combine the meat, Worcestershire, salt, black pepper, paprika, granulated garlic, and scallions.
- Shape the mixture into 8 balls. Then, preheat your Air Fryer to 370 degrees F. Cook for 15 minutes, shaking once or twice.
- Divide the sausage balls, ketchup, mustard, pickled cucumbers, and chopped onion among four serving plates. Bon appétit!

Per serving: 256 Calories; 9.9g Fat; 5.2g Carbs; 35.5g Protein;

34. Family Grilled Beef Sirloin

(Ready in about 25 minutes | Servings 4)

INGREDIENTS

1 ¼ pounds beef sirloin, trim off ex-
    cess fat and silver skin
1 tablespoon cider vinegar
2 garlic cloves, finely minced

1 teaspoon fresh ginger, grated
Sea salt and coarsely ground black
    pepper, to taste
1/2 teaspoon smoked cayenne pepper

DIRECTIONS

- Cut the beef sirloin into steaks.
- In a small mixing bowl, whisk the vinegar, garlic, ginger, salt, black pepper, and cayenne. Massage this rub mixture into the meat; let it marinate for 2 hours in your refrigerator.
- Preheat your Air Fryer to 400 degrees F for 5 to 10 minutes. Insert the Air Fryer grill
  pan.
- Place the prepared sirloin in the grill pan.
- Cook for 14 minutes or until a meat thermometer inserted in the center reaches 160
  degrees F. Bon appétit!

Per serving: 266 Calories; 8.8g Fat; 0.5g Carbs; 43.1g Protein;

35. Herbed Beef Eye Round Roast

(Ready in about 45 minutes + marinating time | Servings 4)

INGREDIENTS

1 tablespoon fresh lime juice

1 ½ tablespoons sesame oil

1/2 teaspoon mustard seeds

1 sprig thyme, leaves picked and chopped

2 sprigs rosemary, leaves picked and chopped

Salt and coarsely ground black pepper, to your liking

1 ½ pounds beef eye round roast, trim off excess fat

DIRECTIONS

- Preheat your Air Fryer to 380 degrees F. Mix the fresh lime juice, sesame oil, mustard seeds, thyme, rosemary, salt, and black pepper.
- Massage the rub mix into the beef eye round roast; wrap it in a saran wrap and place in the refrigerator for 2 hours.
- Cook for 45 minutes, flipping halfway through the cooking time. Check for doneness and let it rest for a couple of minutes before slicing and serving.
- Cut across the grain and serve. Bon appétit!

Per serving: 293 Calories; 12.3g Fat; 0.5g Carbs; 42.5g Protein;

36. Sirloin Steaks with Roasted Zucchini

(Ready in about 25 minutes + marinating time | Servings 4)

INGREDIENTS

4 sirloin steaks

1/4 cup apple cider vinegar

2 tablespoons tamari sauce

1 teaspoon grated ginger

2 tablespoons scallions, chopped

2 garlic cloves, minced

2 tablespoons sesame oil

Salt and ground black pepper, to taste

1 teaspoon paprika

1 pound zucchini, sliced

1 tablespoon olive oil

DIRECTIONS

- Place the sirloin steaks, apple cider vinegar, tamari sauce, grated ginger, scallions, garlic, sesame oil, salt, pepper, and paprika in a mixing dish.
- Wrap with a piece of foil and let it marinate at least 2 hours in the refrigerator.
- Preheat the Air Fryer to 400 degrees F. Cook for 13 minutes, working in batches. Reserve, keeping warm.
- Place the zucchini in the cooking basket. Sprinkle the zucchini with salt and pepper to taste; drizzle with olive oil. Cook at 400 degrees F for 12 minutes, shaking halfway through the cooking time.
- Serve with the sirloin steaks. Bon appétit!

Per serving: 371 Calories; 17.1g Fat; 6g Carbs; 47.6g Protein;

37. Steak Fingers with Pickle Sauce

(Ready in about 20 minutes | Servings 6)

INGREDIENTS

1/2 cup pork rinds

1/2 cup Romano cheese, grated

1 teaspoon paprika

1 teaspoon thyme

Salt and ground black pepper, to your liking

3/4 cup water

2 eggs

1 ½ pounds cube steak, cut into 1-inch strips

1/2 cup mayo

2 tablespoons sour cream

1 pickled cucumber, finely chopped

1 garlic clove, minced

DIRECTIONS

- Mix the pork rinds with the Romano cheese, paprika, thyme, salt, ground black pepper and water in a shallow bowl; add the eggs and mix to combine well.
- Tenderize the cube steak by pounding with a mallet.
- Dip the beef pieces into the breadcrumb/egg mixture and coat on all sides.
- Cook at 380 degrees F Cook for 14 minutes, flipping halfway through the cooking time.
- Meanwhile, make the sauce by mixing mayo with sour cream, pickled cucumber, and minced garlic. Serve with the prepared beef.

Per serving: 411 Calories; 29.8g Fat; 2.5g Carbs; 33.1g Protein;

38. Extraordinary Beef Koftas with Cauli "Rice"

(Ready in about 25 minutes | Servings 4)

INGREDIENTS

2 cups cauliflower florets

3/4 pound ground chuck

1 shallot, finely chopped

2 garlic cloves, finely minced

1 teaspoon brown sugar

1 teaspoon paprika

2 tablespoons flaxseed meal

Sea salt and ground black pepper, to taste

1/2 teaspoon ground cumin

5 saffron threads

1 ½ tablespoons loosely packed fresh continental parsley leaves

DIRECTIONS

- Pulse the cauliflower in a food processor; process until broken down into rice-size pieces.
- Heat the olive oil in a pan; now, cook the cauliflower over medium heat for about 4 minutes or until heated through; fluff the cauli "rice" with a fork.
- Add the remaining ingredients; mix until everything is well incorporated.
- Now, mound a tablespoonful of the meat mixture around a wooden skewer into a pointed-ended sausage using your hands.
- Cook in the preheated Air Fryer for 25 minutes at 360 degrees F. Serve and enjoy!

Per serving: 175 Calories; 8.9g Fat; 6g Carbs; 18.9g Protein;

39. Crispy Beef Schnitzel

(Ready in about 20 minutes | Servings 2)

INGREDIENTS

2 beef schnitzel

1 paprika, or more to taste

1/2 teaspoon sea salt

1/4 freshly ground black pepper, or
more to taste

1/3 cup Parmesan cheese, preferably
freshly grated

2 tablespoons olive oil

1 egg

2 tablespoons fresh cilantro, roughly
chopped

DIRECTIONS

- Preheat your Air Fryer to 390 degrees F for 5 to 10 minutes.
- Season the beef schnitzels with paprika, salt, and ground black pepper.
- In a shallow dish, combine the buttered crumbs with the oil. In a separate shallow dish, whisk the egg until pale and frothy.
- Now, coat the beef schnitzels with the beaten egg; then, coat it with Parmesan cheese.
- Cook for 12 minutes, flipping halfway through the cooking time. Serve warm, garnished with fresh cilantro. Bon appétit!

Per serving: 447 Calories; 29.9g Fat; 2.5g Carbs; 42.3g Protein;

40. Favorite Family Picadillo

(Ready in about 25 minutes | Servings 4)

INGREDIENTS

1 ½ tablespoons olive oil

1 pound ground chuck

2 bell peppers, chopped

1 onion, chopped

2 garlic cloves, minced

1/4 cup pimento stuffed olives

2 tomatoes, chopped

2 tablespoons alcaparrado

1 teaspoon ground cumin

Coarse salt and ground black pepper
   to taste

DIRECTIONS

- Start by preheating your Air Fryer to 380 degrees F.
- Add the olive oil, ground chuck, bell peppers, onion and garlic to the Air Fryer baking pan. Cook for 9 minutes.
- Add the remaining ingredients and cook for a further 15 minutes. Taste, adjust the seasonings, and serve warm.
- Bon appétit!

Per serving: 249 Calories; 14g Fat; 6.2g Carbs; 23.8g Protein;

41. Ribeye with Mustard and Beer Sauce

(Ready in about 20 minutes | Servings 4)

INGREDIENTS

1 pound ribeye

2 teaspoons yellow mustard

2 tablespoons onion, minced

2 garlic cloves, minced

1 tablespoon fresh parsley, chopped

1 ¼ cups dark beer

2 tablespoons lemon juice

2 bay leaves

1 ½ tablespoons olive oil

Salt and ground black pepper, to your
liking

DIRECTIONS

- Place all ingredients in a mixing dish; let it marinate overnight in the refrigerator.
- Discard the marinade.
- Cook the ribeye in the preheated Air Fryer at 400 degrees F for 15 minutes.
- In the meantime, cook the marinade in a pan that is preheated over a moderately high heat. You can add 1 tablespoon of flaxseed meal to thicken the sauce.
- Cook until the sauce is reduced by half. Serve the rib eye with the sauce on the side. Bon appétit!

Per serving: 235 Calories; 10.4g Fat; 4.3g Carbs; 26.3g Protein;

42. Lebanese-Style Beef Strips with Horseradish Sauce

(Ready in about 25 minutes | Servings 4)

INGREDIENTS

1 pound beef tenderloin, cut into
  strips
1/2 cup arrowroot powder
1 teaspoon Seven-spice powder
1 cup buttermilk
Kosher salt and ground black pepper,
  to taste

For the Sauce:
1/2 cup sour cream
2 tablespoons grated fresh horseradish
1 teaspoon stone ground mustard
Sea salt and freshly ground black pepper, to taste

DIRECTIONS

- Pat dry the beef and set it aside.
- In a shallow dish, combine the arrowroot and Seven-spice powder. Add the buttermilk with the salt, and black pepper to another shallow dish.
- Dip the beef strips in the arrowroot mixture. Then, dip into the buttermilk mixture; coat them again with the arrowroot mixture on all sides.
- Preheat your Air Fryer to 370 degrees F. Grease the inside of a cooking basket using an oil mister. Now, cook the beef for 14 minutes, shaking the cooking basket once or twice.
- Meanwhile, make the horseradish sauce by mixing all of the sauce ingredients.
- Serve the warm beef strips with the prepared horseradish sauce on the side. Bon appétit!

Per serving: 319 Calories; 13.9g Fat; 5.9g Carbs; 38.4g Protein;

FISH & SEAFOOD

43. Easy Sunday Shrimp

(Ready in about 15 minutes | Servings 4)

INGREDIENTS

1 pound shrimp, veins and shells re-
    moved and washed
2 tablespoons dry white wine
3 tablespoons good olive oil
Sea salt and freshly ground black
    pepper

1 teaspoon paprika
2 eggs
1 cup Parmesan cheese, grated

DIRECTIONS

- Drizzle the shrimp with the dry white wine and olive oil. Season with salt, pepper, and paprika to taste.
- Beat the eggs in a shallow bowl. Place the dried bread flakes in another shallow bowl.
- Dip your shrimp in egg, then, in the grated parmesan cheese.
- Now, preheat the Air Fryer to 360 degrees F. Cook the shrimp for 7 minutes, flipping halfway through the cooking time.
- Bon appétit!

Per serving: 330 Calories; 19.8g Fat; 4.1g Carbs; 32.7g Protein;

44. Ginger Lime Glazed Salmon Steaks

(Ready in about 15 minutes + marinating time | Servings 4)

INGREDIENTS

4 (2-inch thick) salmon steaks

1/2 teaspoon fresh ginger, grated

1 tablespoon Worcestershire sauce

2 tablespoons lime juice

1 teaspoon garlic, minced

1 tablespoon sesame oil

1/2 teaspoon smoked cayenne pepper

1/4 teaspoon dried dill

1/2 teaspoon dried rosemary

1/2 teaspoon sea salt

1/4 teaspoon ground black pepper, or
   more to taste

DIRECTIONS

- Preheat your Air Fryer to 380 degrees F. Pat dry the salmon steaks with a kitchen towel.
- In a mixing dish, combine the remaining ingredients until everything is well whisked. Add the salmon steaks and wrap with a piece of foil.
- Transfer to the refrigerator for 2 hours. Discard the marinade and place the salmon steaks in the cooking basket.
- Cook for 12 minutes, flipping halfway through the cooking time.
- Meanwhile, cook the marinade in a saucepan that is preheated over a moderate heat. Cook until the sauce is thickened.
- Pour the sauce over the steaks and serve with green salad. Bon appétit!

Per serving: 210 Calories; 11.5g Fat; 1.7g Carbs; 23.4g Protein;

45. Easy Aromatic Cod Filets

(Ready in about 20 minutes | Servings 4)

INGREDIENTS

2 eggs

2 tablespoons olive oil

1 cup almond flour

1 teaspoon sumac

1 teaspoon turmeric

Salt and ground black pepper, to your liking

4 cod filets

2 tablespoons fresh mint leaves, chopped

DIRECTIONS

- Begin by preheating your Air Fryer to 380 degrees F.
- In a shallow bowl, beat the eggs until frothy.
- In another shallow mixing bowl, combine the oil, almond flour, sumac, turmeric, salt, and black pepper.
- Dip each cod fillet into the beaten eggs. Then, coat with the nacho chips mixture until they are covered on all sides.
- Transfer to a cooking basket and cook for 10 minutes or until the fish is thoroughly cooked. Serve garnished with fresh mint leaves. Enjoy!

Per serving: 212 Calories; 12.2g Fat; 2.1g Carbs; 22.1g Protein;

46. Surimi and Ricotta Wontons

(Ready in about 30 minutes | Servings 5)

INGREDIENTS

5 ounces Ricotta cheese, at room temperature

2 tablespoons sour cream

2 tablespoons scallions, chopped

1 teaspoon oyster sauce

5 sticks of surimi, chopped up

1/3 teaspoon sea salt

Lemon pepper, to taste

10 pieces chicken skin

DIRECTIONS

- Blitz the Ricotta, sour cream, scallion, and oyster sauce in your food processor. Transfer to a mixing bowl.
- Add the surimi, salt, and lemon pepper to taste; mix to combine.
- Divide the mixture among the chicken skin wonton wrappers. Cook in the preheated Air Fryer at 390 degrees F for 10 minutes; work in batches.
- Transfer to a serving platter and serve with a dipping sauce of choice. Bon appétit!

Per serving: 252 Calories; 19.4g Fat; 4.8g Carbs; 14.2g Protein;

47. King Prawns alla Parmigiana

(Ready in about 15 minutes | Servings 4)

INGREDIENTS

3/4 cup almond flour

2 egg whites

1 cup Parmigiano-Reggiano, grated

1/2 teaspoon sea salt

1/2 teaspoon ground black pepper

1 teaspoon garlic powder

1/2 teaspoon shallot powder

1/2 teaspoon dried rosemary

1 pound king prawns

1 fresh lemon, cut into wedges

DIRECTIONS

- To make a breading station, place the flour in a shallow dish. In a separate dish, beat the egg whites.
- In a third dish, place the Parmigiano-Reggiano. Add the seasonings and mix to combine well.
- Dip the prawns in the flour, then into the egg whites; lastly, dip them in the parmesan mixture until they are covered on all sides.
- Preheat your Air Fryer to 390 degrees F and cook your prawns for 5 to 7 minutes or until golden brown. Serve with lemon wedges and enjoy!

Per serving: 225 Calories; 8.6g Fat; 6.6g Carbs; 28.8g Protein;

48. Smoked Haddock Fish Cakes

(Ready in about 15 minutes | Servings 6)

INGREDIENTS

1 pound smoked haddock, cooked

1/2 cup cauliflower rice

3 spring onions, finely chopped

1 handful of cheddar cheese, grated

2 tablespoons fresh parsley leaves,
   chopped

Sea salt and ground black pepper, to
   taste

1 teaspoon lemon zest

1 cup almond flour

DIRECTIONS

- Flake the smoked haddock in a mixing bowl. Add the cauli rice, spring onions, cheddar, parsley, salt, pepper and lemon zest.
- Mix until everything is well combined, avoiding breaking up the haddock too much.
- Form the mixture into 6 patties and coat with almond flour on all sides.
- Now, preheat your Air Fryer to 370 degrees F. Transfer the fish cakes to a cooking basket and spritz them with a nonstick cooking spray.
- Cook for 6 minutes or until they're cooked through. Bon appétit!

Per serving: 245 Calories; 15.7g Fat; 5.5g Carbs; 21.4g Protein;

49. Tilapia Fillets with Sour Cream Sauce

(Ready in about 20 minutes | Servings 4)

INGREDIENTS

2 eggs

1/2 cup crushed tortilla chips

1/2 teaspoon fresh ginger, grated

2 tablespoons fresh cilantro, chopped

1/2 teaspoon sea salt

1/3 teaspoon ground black pepper, to taste

1/2 teaspoon smoked paprika

1/2 teaspoon chipotle powder

4 tilapia fillets

1/2 cup sour cream

2 tablespoons full-fat mayonnaise

1 teaspoon lemon juice

1/2 teaspoon dried dill weed

DIRECTIONS

- Place the eggs in a shallow bowl and whisk until they are frothy.
- In another mixing bowl, place the crushed tortilla chips, ginger, cilantro, salt, black pepper, paprika, and chipotle powder.
- Dip the tilapia fillets in the beaten eggs, and then, in the tortilla chips mixture. Cook in the preheated Air Fryer at 380 degrees F for 13 minutes.
- Thoroughly combine the sour cream, mayonnaise, lemon juice, and dill weed. Serve with the tilapia fillets. Bon appétit!

Per serving: 310 Calories; 14.1g Fat; 6.6g Carbs; 36.5g Protein;

50. Last Minute Cod Fillets

(Ready in about 15 minutes + marinating time | Servings 4)

INGREDIENTS

4 cod fillets

1/2 teaspoon seasoned salt

1/2 teaspoon white pepper

1 teaspoon granulated garlic

1 teaspoon onion powder

1/2 teaspoon orange zest

1/2 cup tamari sauce

2 tablespoons peanut oil

1 lime, cut into wedges

DIRECTIONS

- Sprinkle the cod fillets with the seasoned salt, pepper, garlic, and onion powder.
- In a mixing bowl, thoroughly combine the orange zest, tamari sauce, and peanut oil. Place the fish in this sauce.
- Allow it to marinate for 2 hours in the refrigerator.
- Preheat your Air Fryer to 380 degrees for 5 minutes. Cook the fish fillets for 12 minutes. Serve with lime wedges. Bon appétit!

Per serving: 156 Calories; 7.3g Fat; 4.1g Carbs; 18.4g Protein;

51. Old Bay Calamari with Hot Mayo Sauce

(Ready in about 20 minutes | Servings 4)

INGREDIENTS

1 pound squid, cleaned and cut into
rings and tentacle pieces
3/4 cup almond flour
2 eggs
1 tablespoon Old Bay seasoning
Sea salt and ground black pepper, to
taste
1 teaspoon shallot powder
1/2 cup parmesan cheese, grated
Coconut oil, place in an oil mister

For the sauce:
1/2 cup mayonnaise
2 tablespoons sour cream
1 teaspoon Sriracha

DIRECTIONS

- Preheat your Air Fryer to 390 degrees F.
- Rinse the squid and pat it dry. Place the flour in a shallow bowl.
- In another bowl, whisk the eggs with the Old Bay seasoning, salt, black pepper, and shallot powder.
- Add the parmesan cheese to a third shallow bowl.
- Dredge the squid pieces in the flour. Then, dip them into the egg mixture; afterwards, cover with the parmesan cheese.
- Arrange the squids in the cooking basket. Spritz them with coconut oil and cook for 8 to 12 minutes, depending on the desired level of doneness. Work in batches.
- Then, make the sauce by whisking all of the sauce ingredients. Serve with the warm fried squid and enjoy!

Per serving: 405 Calories; 28.2g Fat; 5.7g Carbs; 28g Protein;

52. Bay Scallops with Ketchup Mayonnaise Sauce

(Ready in about 15 minutes | Servings 4)

INGREDIENTS

For the Scallops:

1 pound bay scallops

1 ½ tablespoons extra-virgin olive oil

1 teaspoon cayenne pepper

1 teaspoon shallot powder

1/2 teaspoon ground bay leaf

1 teaspoon granulated garlic

Sea salt and ground black pepper, to taste

1/2 teaspoon dried rosemary

1 teaspoon dried basil

1/2 teaspoon chipotle powder

For the Dipping Sauce:

1/2 cup mayonnaise

1/4 cup tomato ketchup

1 tablespoon Worcestershire sauce

1/4 teaspoon ground black pepper

DIRECTIONS

- Wash the scallops and pat them dry. Transfer them to a re-sealable zipper storage bag.
- Add the remaining ingredients for the scallops and shake until the scallops are covered with seasonings on all sides.
- Preheat your Air Fryer to 400 degrees F. Cook for 7 minutes, shaking halfway through the cooking time.
- In the meantime, make the sauce by mixing the mayonnaise, ketchup, Worcestershire sauce, and ground black pepper. Serve with the prepared scallops and enjoy!

Per serving: 291 Calories; 23.4g Fat; 4.9g Carbs; 14g Protein;

53. Tuna Steak in Beer Sauce

(Ready in about 20 minutes | Servings 4)

INGREDIENTS

4 tuna steaks

Sea salt and ground black pepper, to taste

1 teaspoon cayenne pepper

1 cup beer

1/4 cup Worcestershire sauce

2 tablespoons safflower oil

2 tablespoons arrowroot powder

3 tablespoons water

DIRECTIONS

- Place the tuna steaks in a mixing bowl. Add the other ingredients and let it marinate for 1 hour in your refrigerator.
- Preheat your Air Fryer to 390 degrees F. Cook for 10 minutes or until the tuna flakes easily with a fork.
- In the meantime, preheat a medium-sized saucepan over a moderate flame. Cook the marinade until it is reduced by half.
- Pour the sauce over the prepared tuna steaks and serve immediately. Bon appétit!

Per serving: 278 Calories; 12.5g Fat; 6.9g Carbs; 26.7g Protein;

54. Crab Tacos with Mexican Hot Sauce

(Ready in about 15 minutes | Servings 4)

INGREDIENTS

1 cup Cheddar cheese, shredded
1/2 cup milk
1 egg, beaten
1 cup almond flour
Salt and ground black pepper, to taste
12 softshell crabs, cleaned

For the Sauce:
1 teaspoon Mexican hot sauce
1/2 cup mayonnaise
1 tablespoon pickles, chopped
2 tablespoons scallions, chopped
1 garlic clove, minced

DIRECTIONS

- Start by preheating your oven to 350 degrees F.
- On a baking sheet lined with parchment paper place 1/4 cup of the cheese. Press them down to make a tortilla shape.
- Bake for 5 to 7 minutes or until the edges of the cheese are delicately browned. Let the cheese tortillas cool for 2 to 3 minutes.
- Then, preheat your Air Fryer to 390 degrees F for 5 to 10 minutes.
- In a bowl, mix the milk, egg, flour, salt, and ground black pepper. Dip the softshell crabs in the batter and transfer them to the cooking basket.
- Cook for 6 minutes or until they are thoroughly cooked.
- Then, in a mixing bowl, thoroughly combine the Asian hot sauce, mayonnaise, pickles, scallions, and minced garlic.
- Assemble your tacos with the crab, sauce, and tortillas. Bon appétit!

Per serving: 605 Calories; 52.5g Fat; 5.8g Carbs; 24.6g Protein;

55. Cajun Fish Burger Bowls

(Ready in about 15 minutes | Servings 4)

Per serving: 221 Calories; 12.9g Fat; 3.8g Carbs; 21.3g Protein;

INGREDIENTS

1 pound sole fish, chopped

1 teaspoon Cajun spice mix

1 shallot, finely chopped

1 garlic clove, minced

1 egg

2 tablespoons buttermilk

1/2 cup parmesan cheese, grated

1 handful mixed lettuce

4 tablespoons mayonnaise

DIRECTIONS

- Add the sole fish, Cajun spice mix, shallot, garlic, egg and buttermilk to your food processor; process until everything is well combined.
- Place the cheese in a shallow dish.
- Shape the mixture into 4 patties; coat each patty with cheese. Cook the fish burgers in the preheated Air Fryer at 390 degrees F for 8 minutes.
- Afterwards, assemble the bowls with the mixed lettuce, fish patties and mayonnaise. Bon appétit!

56. Grilled and Ginger-Glazed Halibut Steak

(Ready in about 25 minutes | Servings 2)

Per serving: 529 Calories; 43.8g Fat; 6.5g Carbs; 24.9g Protein;

INGREDIENTS

1/2 cup ketchup

3 tablespoons olive oil

1 tablespoon lemon juice

1/2 teaspoon fresh ginger, grated

2 tablespoons Erythritol

1 teaspoon onion powder

1 teaspoon dried parsley flakes

1 teaspoon garlic, minced

Salt and freshly ground black pepper, to taste

2 (2-inch thick) halibut steaks

DIRECTIONS

- Place all of the above ingredients in a mixing dish; wrap with foil and transfer to your refrigerator. Allow it to marinate for 1 hour.
- In the meantime, preheat your Air Fryer to 400 degrees F. Remove the halibut steaks from the marinade and cook them for 10 minutes or until they are opaque throughout.
- Next, preheat a medium-sized saucepan over a moderate flame. Cook the marinade until it is reduced by half.
- Pour the glaze over the fish. Place under a broiler for 5 minutes or until the halibut steaks are browned. Eat warm. Bon appétit!

VEGETABLES & SIDE DISHES

57. Hot and Spicy Broccoli with Peppers

(Ready in about 20 minutes | Servings 4)

INGREDIENTS

1 pound broccoli, broken into florets

1 bell pepper, chopped

1 serrano pepper, chopped

2 tablespoons butter, melted

2 spring onions, chopped

2 cloves garlic, minced

1 tablespoon coconut aminos

Sea salt and ground black pepper, to taste

1/2 teaspoon cayenne pepper

1/2 teaspoon chipotle powder

DIRECTIONS

- Preheat your Air Fryer to 400 degrees F.
- Brush the broccoli and peppers with melted butter and transfer to a cooking basket.
- Add the peppers to the preheated Air Fryer and cook for 9 minutes, shaking once or twice. Add the remaining ingredients, along with the broccoli.
- Cook an additional 6 minutes. Serve immediately and enjoy!

Per serving: 95 Calories; 6.2g Fat; 6.7g Carbs; 3.5g Protein;

58. Bok Choy Salad with Montrachet

(Ready in about 50 minutes + chilling time | Servings 4)

INGREDIENTS

1 pound Bok choy

1/4 cup extra-virgin olive oil

2 teaspoons Dijon mustard

2 tablespoons balsamic vinegar

Coarse salt and freshly ground black
    pepper, to taste

2 cups baby arugula

2 cloves garlic, minced

4 ounces Montrachet cheese, crum-
    bled

DIRECTIONS

- Preheat your Air Fryer to 390 degrees F.
- Cook your Bok choy for 10 minutes, turning halfway through the cooking time. Cut the Bok choy into thin slices using a sharp kitchen knife; transfer to a salad bowl.
- In a small mixing dish, thoroughly combine the olive oil, mustard, balsamic vinegar, salt, and black pepper.
- Toss the Bok choy with the arugula, garlic, and the prepared vinaigrette. Top with the crumbled Montrachet cheese and serve well-chilled. Bon appétit!

Per serving: 207 Calories; 16.2g Fat; 5g Carbs; 10.9g Protein;

59. Roasted Vegetables with Sriracha Mayo

(Ready in about 20 minutes | Servings 4)

INGREDIENTS

2 Roma tomatoes, halved

1/2 pound eggplant, cubed

1/2 pound mushrooms, quartered

1 red onion, sliced

1 teaspoon garlic, minced

1/4 cup butter, melted

1 teaspoon cayenne pepper

1/2 teaspoon dried dill

1/2 teaspoon dried basil

1/2 teaspoon dried rosemary

Salt and ground black pepper, to taste

1/2 cup mayonnaise

1/2 teaspoon Sriracha

DIRECTIONS

- Preheat your Air Fryer to 380 degrees F.
- Spritz the inside of a baking pan with a nonstick cooking spray. Add the vegetables together with the butter and seasonings to the baking pan.
- Place the pan in the Air Fryer and roast the vegetables for 10 minutes.
- Increase the temperature to 400 degrees F. Cook an additional 5 minutes.
- In the meantime, mix the mayonnaise with the Sriracha. Serve with the warm vegetables. Bon appétit!

Per serving: 253 Calories; 23.6g Fat; 7.1g Carbs; 3.5g Protein;

60. Beef and Mushroom Stuffed Zucchini

(Ready in about 35 minutes | Servings 4)

INGREDIENTS

1 pound zucchini, cut in half lengthwise
1 tablespoon olive oil
1 yellow onion, chopped
1/2 pound ground beef
1/2 pound button mushrooms,
   chopped

1 Serrano pepper, chopped
1 teaspoon garlic paste
Salt and ground black pepper, to taste
1 tomato, pureed
1/2 tablespoon soy sauce
1 sprig dried rosemary, leaves picked

DIRECTIONS

- Scoop out the pulp of the zucchini with a teaspoon, leaving 1/2-inch shells. Finely chop the pulp.
- Preheat the oil in a sauté pan over a moderate heat. Now, sweat the onion for 2 to 3 minutes.
- Add the ground beef, mushrooms, Serrano pepper and garlic paste; continue to cook an additional 4 minutes. Sprinkle with salt and pepper; cover and set it aside.
- Add the pureed tomato, soy sauce, and dried rosemary. Add the zucchini pulp and mix to combine.
- Divide the mixture among the zucchini boats and transfer them to a lightly greased baking pan.
- Next, preheat your Air Fryer to 400 degrees F. Place the baking pan in your Air Fryer and bake for 17 minutes. Serve warm. Bon appétit!

Per serving: 215 Calories; 13.6g Fat; 6.6g Carbs; 16.6g Protein;

61. Easy Cauliflower Au Gratin

(Ready in about 40 minutes | Servings 6)

INGREDIENTS

1 ½ pounds cauliflower, cut into florets
1/2 cup onion, chopped
1 tablespoon butter, softened
1 cup milk

2 cups Cheddar cheese, shredded
Kosher salt and ground black pepper,
   to taste

DIRECTIONS

- Place a steamer insert into a pan and fill with water. Bring the water to a boil. Then, steam the cauliflower for 6 minutes.
- Then, preheat the Air Fryer to 400 degrees F.
- Arrange the cauliflower in a lightly greased baking pan. Top with the chopped onion.
- In a mixing dish, thoroughly combine the butter, milk, cheese, salt and black pepper. Pour the mixture over the cauliflower in the baking pan. Cook for 20 minutes in your Air Fryer.
- Scatter the cheese over the top and cook an additional 12 minutes or until the cheese has melted. Enjoy!

Per serving: 247 Calories; 17.5g Fat; 6.5g Carbs; 14.7g Protein;

62. Cheesy Veggie Fried Balls

(Ready in about 30 minutes | Servings 5)

INGREDIENTS

2 cups zucchini, grated

1 cup cauliflower, riced

1 cup Romano cheese, freshly grated

1 ½ cups Colby cheese, freshly grated

1/2 teaspoon dried dill weed

1 teaspoon garlic powder

1 teaspoon paprika

Salt and pepper, to taste

1 egg, beaten

DIRECTIONS

- Mix all of the above ingredients until everything is well incorporated.
- Take 1 tablespoon of the veggie mixture and roll into a ball. Transfer it to the preheated Air Fryer.
- Repeat until you run out of ingredients. Cook at 360 degrees F for 15 minutes or until thoroughly cooked and crispy.
- Work in batches and transfer to a nice serving platter. Bon appétit!

Per serving: 281 Calories; 21.7g Fat; 4.1g Carbs; 17.8g Protein;

63. Crispy Zucchini with Ranch Dressing

(Ready in about 30 minutes | Servings 5)

INGREDIENTS

2 eggs

1/4 cup buttermilk

1 teaspoon dried thyme

1/2 teaspoon dried oregano

1/2 teaspoon dried basil

1/2 teaspoon garlic powder

1 cup Romano cheese, grated

1 cup Asiago cheese, freshly grated

1 pound zucchini, peeled and quartered lengthwise

1 cup ranch dressing

DIRECTIONS

- Preheat your Air Fryer to 400 degrees F.
- In a shallow dish, whisk the eggs with buttermilk until frothy.
- Then, place the thyme, oregano, basil, garlic powder, Romano and Asiago cheese in a separate bowl.
- Dip each piece of the zucchini in the egg/buttermilk mixture; then, roll them into the cheese/chips mixture.
- Arrange the zucchinis in a cooking basket and brush them with olive oil. Cook for 12 minutes, shaking halfway through the cooking time.
- Work in batches and transfer to a serving platter. Serve with ranch dressing. Enjoy!

Per serving: 435 Calories; 37.1g Fat; 6.6g Carbs; 17.9g Protein;

64. Jicama Fries with Greek Dipping Sauce

(Ready in about 30 minutes | Servings 4)

INGREDIENTS

1 pound jicama, trimmed and slice
   into sticks
1 teaspoon coarse salt
1/4 teaspoon grated nutmeg
2 tablespoons olive oil
The Sauce:

1/2 cup full-fat Greek yogurt
1 teaspoon lemon juice
1/2 teaspoon sea salt
1 teaspoon garlic, minced
1/2 teaspoon black pepper, freshly
   cracked

DIRECTIONS

- Place the jicama sticks in the cooking basket in a single layer. Sprinkle with salt and nutmeg. Drizzle with olive oil.
- Cook in the preheated Air Fryer at 400 degrees F for 4 to 5 minutes. Work in batches and give them a shake twice during cooking.
- Meanwhile, make the Greek dipping sauce by mixing the yogurt, lemon juice, sea salt, garlic and pepper.
- Serve with roasted carrots and enjoy!

Per serving: 111 Calories; 7.8g Fat; 7g Carbs; 1.6g Protein;

65. Classic Roasted Brussels Sprouts

(Ready in about 20 minutes | Servings 4)

INGREDIENTS

3/4 pound Brussels sprouts

2 tablespoons olive oil

1 teaspoon coarse salt

1/2 teaspoon ground black pepper

1/2 teaspoon smoked paprika

DIRECTIONS

- Preheat your Air Fryer to 380 degrees F.
- Toss the Brussels sprouts with the olive oil, salt, black pepper, and paprika.
- Cook for 15 minutes or until they are crisp-tender, shaking twice during cooking.
- Serve warm with your favorite dipping sauce. Bon appétit!

Per serving: 96 Calories; 7g Fat; 6.2g Carbs; 2.9g Protein;

66. Cauliflower and Onion Pakoras

(Ready in about 20 minutes | Servings 4)

INGREDIENTS

1 ½ cups cauliflower, chopped

1/2 onion, finely chopped

1 garlic clove, minced

1 teaspoon fresh ginger, grated

Salt and ground black pepper, to taste

1 teaspoon paprika

1 teaspoon curry powder

1/2 teaspoon garam masala

1 cup almond flour

1/2 teaspoon baking powder

1 tablespoon olive oil

Water, as needed

DIRECTIONS

- Add the cauliflower, onion, garlic and ginger to a mixing bowl. Now, sprinkle, with salt, pepper, paprika, curry powder, and garam masala; stir to combine well.
- Now, stir in the flour and baking powder; mix again.
- Add the olive oil; then, pour in water until soft dough forms. The mixture should not be too thick. Actually, you would be able to form the mixture into patties.
- Preheat your Air Fryer to 380 degrees F. Place the prepared patties in your Air Fryer and cook for 15 minutes, turning halfway through the cooking time. Bon appétit!

Per serving: 184 Calories; 15.4g Fat; 5.6g Carbs; 5.9g Protein;

67. Korokke with Cheddar cheese

(Ready in about 1 hour | Servings 5)

INGREDIENTS

3/4 pound kohlrabi stems and roots removed

2 eggs, whisked

8 ounces Cheddar cheese, preferably freshly grated

1/2 cup almond flour

1/2 teaspoon seasoned salt

1/3 teaspoon ground black pepper

4 ounces Parmesan cheese, grated

Tonkatsu sauce, to serve

DIRECTIONS

- Place the kohlrabi in a pan of boiling water; simmer for 20 to 25 minutes.
- Mash the kohlrabi and allow them to cool completely. Stir in the eggs, Cheddar cheese, almond flour, salt, and black pepper.
- Shape the mixture into 4 cakes and cover with the grated parmesan cheese.
- Preheat your Air Fryer to 390 degrees F. Cook for 10 minutes or until brown on the outside. Serve with Tonkatsu sauce if desired. Enjoy!

Per serving: 378 Calories; 28.1g Fat; 5.8g Carbs; 22.7g Protein;

68. Parmesan Green Beans with Wasabi Sauce

(Ready in about 20 minutes | Servings 4)

INGREDIENTS

1 pound green beans

1 tablespoon sesame oil

1/2 cup parmesan cheese, grated

1 teaspoon paprika

Seasoned salt to taste ground black
  pepper, to taste

For the Sauce:

1/2 cup sour cream

1 teaspoon wasabi paste

Salt, to taste

DIRECTIONS

- Bring a lightly salted water to a boil; boil the green beans for 2 minutes. Now, drain the green beans and dry them on a kitchen towel. Drizzle with sesame oil.
- In a mixing bowl, thoroughly combine the parmesan cheese, paprika, salt, and black pepper. Dip the green beans in this mixture, coating all sides.
- Cook the green beans in your Air Fryer at 390 degrees F for 10 minutes.
- Then, whisk the sour cream with the wasabi paste and salt to make the sauce. Serve with the fried green beans and enjoy!

Per serving: 149 Calories; 10.4g Fat; 6.3g Carbs; 5.9g Protein;

69. Mediterranean-Style Vegetable Rounds
(Ready in about 30 minutes | Servings 4)

INGREDIENTS

1 (1 1/4-pound) eggplant, slice into
   1-inch thick rounds
1 red onion, sliced
2 tablespoons butter, melted
Sea salt and ground black pepper, to
   taste

1/2 teaspoon dried oregano
1/2 teaspoon garlic powder
1/2 teaspoon dried basil
1/2 teaspoon dried rosemary
1/4 teaspoon dried thyme

DIRECTIONS

- Preheat your Air Fryer to 380 degrees F.
- Brush the eggplants and onion with the melted butter. Now, toss them with the seasoning until they are well covered.
- Arrange the slices of eggplant in the cooking basket; cook for 20 minutes, flipping halfway through the cooking time.
- Now, add the slices of onion and cook an additional 10 minutes. Serve immediately and enjoy!

Per serving: 96 Calories; 6.1g Fat; 5.9g Carbs; 1.4g Protein;

70. Broccoli Stuffed Mushrooms with Cheese

(Ready in about 15 minutes | Servings 4)

INGREDIENTS

8 large white button mushrooms,
   cleaned and stems removed
1 cup broccoli, chopped
1 cup Pepper-Jack cheese grated
2 tablespoons scallions, minced
2 garlic cloves, minced

1 teaspoon paprika
Salt and ground black pepper, to your
   liking
1/4 cup fresh Italian parsley leaves,
   chopped

DIRECTIONS

- Give the mushrooms a quick shower and pat them dry as best as you can.
- In a mixing bowl, thoroughly combine the broccoli with the cheese, scallions, garlic, paprika, salt and black pepper.
- Then, divide the mixture among the mushroom caps.
- Preheat your Air Fryer to 390 degrees F. Cook your mushrooms for 8 minutes or until they are thoroughly cooked.
- Transfer the mushrooms to a serving platter, garnish with the Italian parsley and serve.

Per serving: 131 Calories; 9.1g Fat; 4.5g Carbs; 9.1g Protein;

FAST SNACKS & APPETIZERS

71. Garlic and Oregano Bites

(Ready in about 10 minutes | Servings 2)

INGREDIENTS

3/4 pound cauliflower, broken into florets

2 tablespoons extra-virgin olive oil

1/4 teaspoon sea salt

1/2 teaspoon oregano

1 teaspoon granulated garlic

DIRECTIONS

- Toss the cauliflower with the olive oil, salt, oregano, and garlic.
- Preheat the Air Fryer to 400 degrees F. Cook for 9 minutes or until golden brown, shaking halfway through the cooking time.
- Serve and enjoy!

Per serving: 166 Calories; 14.4g Fat; 6.4g Carbs; 3.2g Protein;

72. Baked Avocado Chips

(Ready in about 25 minutes | Servings 2)

INGREDIENTS

1 large ripe avocado, mashed
1 tablespoon freshly squeezed lemon
  juice
1 teaspoon avocado oil
1/4 teaspoon ground cloves
1/2 cup Parmesan cheese, freshly
  grated

1/2 teaspoon garlic powder
1/2 teaspoon Italian seasoning
Kosher salt and ground black pepper,
  to taste

DIRECTIONS

- Mix all of the above ingredients.
- Divide the mixture into balls; flatten each ball with a fork and transfer them to a foil-lined baking pan.
- Put the baking pan into the Air Fryer and bake your chips
- Preheat your Air Fryer to 320 degrees F. Bake for 15 minutes, flipping them over around halfway through the cooking time. Bon appétit!

Per serving: 129 Calories; 9.4g Fat; 4.1g Carbs; 7.1g Protein;

73. Swiss Chard Chips with Avocado Dip

(Ready in about 15 minutes | Servings 6)

INGREDIENTS

1 pound Swiss chard, ribs cut out

2 tablespoons sesame oil

Salt and ground black pepper, to taste

1 teaspoon garlic powder

1 teaspoon cayenne pepper

For the Dipping Sauce:

1 avocado, peeled an pitted

1/2 cup sour cream

2 tablespoons fresh chives, chopped

1 tablespoon fresh lemon juice

1 teaspoon chili pepper, deveined and minced

Sea salt, to taste

DIRECTIONS

- Toss the Swiss chard with the sesame oil, salt, black pepper, garlic powder, and cayenne pepper.
- Preheat your Air Fryer to 380 degrees F. Cook for 4 minutes or until crisp, shaking halfway through the cooking time.
- In the meantime, blitz the avocado, sour cream, chives, lemon juice, chili pepper, and salt in your food processor.
- Process until everything is well blended. Serve with the Swiss chard chips and enjoy!

Per serving: 135 Calories; 11.6g Fat; 7.2g Carbs; 2.7g Protein;

74. Famous Buffalo-Style Wings

(Ready in about 45 minutes | Servings 6)

INGREDIENTS

1 cup almond flour

Sea salt and ground black pepper, to taste

1 teaspoon garlic powder

1/2 teaspoon onion powder

1 teaspoon paprika

1 ¼ pounds chicken wings, split at the joint

1/4 cup hot sauce, or to taste

1 teaspoon Worcestershire sauce

1/2 cup Maytag cheese, crumbled

DIRECTIONS

- Preheat your Air Fryer to 380 degrees F.
- In a mixing dish, combine the flour, salt, black pepper, garlic powder, onion powder, and paprika. Now, dredge the wings in the seasoned flour mixture and coat on all sides.
- Transfer the wings to a cooking basket and spritz them with a nonstick cooking spray.
- Cook for 22 minutes in the Preheated Air Fryer or until cooked through. Work in batches until you run out of ingredients.
- Toss the fried chicken wings with the hot sauce and Worcestershire sauce. Scatter the crumbled cheese over the warm wings and serve immediately. Bon appétit!

Per serving: 295 Calories; 20.5g Fat; 3g Carbs; 25.3g Protein;

75. Zucchini Chips with Chili Mayo

(Ready in about 25 minutes | Servings 6)

INGREDIENTS

2 eggs

2 tablespoons water

1/2 cup Romano cheese, grated

1 ½ tablespoons olive oil

2 zucchinis, peeled and thinly sliced

Sea salt ground black pepper, to taste

1/2 teaspoon cayenne pepper

1/4 cup mayonnaise

1 teaspoon chili sauce

DIRECTIONS

- Whisk the eggs with the water in a shallow dish. Mix the Romano cheese and olive oil in a separate shallow dish.
- Dip the zucchini slices first in the egg wash; then, dredge into the cheese mixture. Sprinkle with salt, black pepper, and cayenne.
- Preheat your Air Fryer to 370 degrees F. Cook for 15 minutes, shaking halfway through the cooking time.
- In a mixing dish, whisk the mayonnaise with the chili sauce. Serve with the zucchini sticks. Bon appétit!

Per serving: 145 Calories; 11.5g Fat; 5.1g Carbs; 6.5g Protein;

76. Cheese-Stuffed Cocktail Meatballs

(Ready in about 15 minutes | Servings 6)

INGREDIENTS

1/2 pound ground beef

1/2 pound sausage, crumbled

1 ¼ cups dried bread flakes

1 garlic clove, minced

Sea salt and ground black pepper, to
taste

1/2 teaspoon hot paprika

1/4 teaspoon ground bay leaf

2 eggs

4 ounces Monterey Jack cheese, cubed

DIRECTIONS

- Preheat your Air Fryer to 380 degrees F.
- In a mixing bowl, thoroughly combine the ground beef, sausage, dried bread flakes, garlic, salt, pepper, paprika, ground bay leaf, and eggs.
- Shape the mixture into meatballs. Add 1 cheese cube to the center of each ball, sealing it inside.
- Spritz the meatballs with a nonstick cooking spray. Cook for 10 minutes, shaking once or twice during the cooking. Serve with cocktail sticks and enjoy!

Per serving: 312 Calories; 20.2g Fat; 5.9g Carbs; 25.3g Protein;

77. Cocktail Lil Smokies

(Ready in about 25 minutes | Servings 8)

INGREDIENTS

1 (28-ounce) package mini smoked
  sausage links

1/2 cup ketchup

1/4 cup dry white wine

1/4 cup water

1 tablespoons stone ground mustard

DIRECTIONS

- Start by preheating your Air Fryer to 380 degrees F.
- Prick the sausages and transfer them to a baking pan. Cook in the preheated Air Fryer for 15 minutes, turning halfway through the cooking time.
- Work in two batches to make sure that sausages don't touch with each other.
- In the meantime, preheat a saucepan over a moderately high flame. Cook the ketchup, wine, water, and mustard until it has thickened.
- Heat off; add the prepared sausages to the saucepan and stir to combine. Serve with toothpicks. Bon appétit!

Per serving: 332 Calories; 28.3g Fat; 5.4g Carbs; 12.2g Protein;

78. Father's Day Crispy Pork Crackling

(Ready in about 25 minutes | Servings 8)

INGREDIENTS

2 sheets of pork skin
1 tablespoon salt
1/2 teaspoon cayenne pepper
1 teaspoon garlic powder
3 tablespoons soy sauce

3 tablespoons fresh lemon juice
1 chili pepper, chopped
2 garlic cloves
1 tablespoon tahini

DIRECTIONS

- Wash the pork skins and prick them (you can use a salami pricker).
- Rub with the salt, cayenne pepper, and garlic powder; place in your refrigerator overnight.
- Preheat your Air Fryer to 400 degrees F. Cook the pork skin on a grill pan for 12 minutes; repeat with the other pork skin.
- Remove from the Air Fryer; cut into strips using kitchen tongs and scissors.
- In the meantime, make the dipping sauce by mixing the remaining ingredients in a food processor. Serve the pork cracklings with the sauce on the side. Enjoy!

Per serving: 268 Calories; 26.7g Fat; 3.4g Carbs; 3.6g Protein;

79. Herbed Tomato Chips with Garlic Mayo

(Ready in about 20 minutes | Servings 4)

INGREDIENTS

3 tomatoes, thinly sliced

3 teaspoons olive oil

Sea salt and ground black pepper, to taste

1 teaspoon dried rosemary, chopped

1 teaspoon dried sage, crushed

1/2 cup full-fat mayonnaise

2 garlic cloves, smashed

1 teaspoon cayenne pepper

DIRECTIONS

- Begin by preheating your Air Fryer to 360 degrees F. Toss the tomato slices with the olive oil, salt, black pepper, rosemary, and sage.
- Cook for 10 minutes, flipping halfway through the cooking time. Meanwhile, mix the mayonnaise, garlic, and cayenne pepper in a bowl.
- Serve the tomato chips with the garlic mayo or store in an airtight container. Bon appétit!

Per serving: 144 Calories; 15g Fat; 2.1g Carbs; 0.5g Protein;

80. Bacon-Wrapped Mushrooms

(Ready in about 20 minutes | Servings 4)

INGREDIENTS

12 medium fresh mushrooms
12 strips of bacon
1/2 cup barbecue sauce

DIRECTIONS

- Start by preheating your Air Fryer to 395 degrees F.
- Wrap each mushroom with a strip of bacon; secure with a toothpick. Arrange the bacon-wrapped mushrooms in a cooking basket. Add the barbecue sauce.
- Cook the bacon-wrapped mushrooms for 10 minutes, flipping them halfway through the cooking time.
- Transfer to a serving platter and enjoy!

Per serving: 365 Calories; 30.9g Fat; 6.1g Carbs; 12.3g Protein;

81. Easy Celery Chips

(Ready in about 20 minutes | Servings 4)

INGREDIENTS

1/4 cup butter, melted

1 teaspoon garlic paste

2 tablespoons coconut amino

Salt and pepper, to taste

2 ½ tablespoons arrowroot powder

1 ½ pounds celery, sliced

DIRECTIONS

- Mix the butter, garlic paste, coconut amino, salt, pepper, and arrowroot in a large bowl. Mix well to form a smooth paste; add a tablespoon of water or two, as needed.
- Add the celery slices to the bowl; mix well until they're coated.
- Now, preheat your Air Fryer to 380 degrees F.
- Cook your veggie chips for 15 minutes, flipping them halfway through the cooking time. Consume within 3 days. Bon appétit!

Per serving: 140 Calories; 11.8g Fat; 5.4g Carbs; 1.8g Protein;

82. The Best Onion Rings Ever

(Ready in about 15 minutes | Servings 6)

INGREDIENTS

1/2 cup Parmesan cheese, grated
1/2 cup pork rinds, crushed
Salt and ground black pepper, to taste
1/2 teaspoon paprika

2 egg whites
2 yellow onions, sliced into rings
2 tablespoons canola oil

DIRECTIONS

- Begin by preheating your Air Fryer to 400 degrees F for 5 minutes.
- Mix the Parmesan cheese, pork rinds, salt, pepper, and paprika. In another bowl, whisk the egg whites.
- Dip the onion rings into the egg whites; then, coat them with the parmesan mixture on all sides. Brush with canola oil and transfer to the Air Fryer cooking basket.
- Cook for 7 minutes, shaking several times during the cooking process; work in batches and serve with your favorite sauce for dipping. Bon appétit!

Per serving: 153 Calories; 11.7g Fat; 5g Carbs; 6.9g Protein;

83. Mozzarella Cheese Sticks

(Ready in about 15 minutes | Servings 4)

INGREDIENTS

1/4 cup almond flour

1/4 cup Parmesan cheese the powdered kind in a can

1 tablespoon coconut flour

1 teaspoon onion powder

1 teaspoon garlic powder

1/2 teaspoon salt

1/2 teaspoon chili flakes

1 egg, beaten

1 (10-ounce) package part skim mozzarella string cheese

DIRECTIONS

- Start by preheating the Air Fryer to 370 degrees F.
- Place the almond flour, Parmesan cheese, coconut flour, onion powder, garlic powder, salt and chili flakes in a zipper sandwich bag. Shake the bag to blend.
- Add the beaten egg. Dip each cheese stick in this mixture. Cook for 5 minutes in the preheated Air Fryer.
- Serve immediately. Bon appétit!

Per serving: 145 Calories; 9g Fat; 7.1g Carbs; 3.4g Protein;

EGGS & DAIRY

84. Classic Deviled Eggs

(Ready in about 20 minutes + chilling time | Servings 3)

INGREDIENTS

6 medium-sized cold eggs

1/4 cup mayonnaise

1 teaspoon Dijon mustard

1 teaspoon rice vinegar

Sea salt and freshly ground black pepper, to taste

Spanish paprika, for garnish

DIRECTIONS

- Place a wire rack inside the air fryer basket; lower the eggs onto the rack.
- Cook at 250 degrees F for 16 minutes.
- Remove the hard-boiled eggs from the Air Fryer and transfer them to a bowl of cold water for 10 minutes. Peel the eggs.
- Slice the eggs in half lengthwise, removing the yolks to a mixing bowl. Then, place the whites on a serving platter.
- Add the mayo, mustard, rice vinegar, salt, and black pepper to the mixing bowl; mix until everything is well incorporated.
- Divide the mixture between the egg whites. Sprinkle with Spanish paprika and serve well chilled. Bon appétit!

Per serving: 191 Calories; 14.7g Fat; 1.3g Carbs; 12.3g Protein;

85. Mushroom and Scallion Omelet

(Ready in about 20 minutes | Servings 2)

INGREDIENTS

4 eggs

1/2 cup milk

1/2 teaspoon sea salt

1/4 teaspoon red pepper flakes, crushed

1 bell pepper, chopped

1/2 cup scallions, chopped

1 cup button mushrooms, chopped

1/2 cup Monterey-Jack cheese, shredded

DIRECTIONS

- Start by preheating the Air Fryer to 360 degrees F.
- Thoroughly combine the eggs and milk using a wire whisk. Sprinkle with salt and red pepper flakes.
- Stir in the vegetables and mix again. Pour the mixture into a baking pan. Place the pan in the air fryer basket.
- Cook approximately 5 minutes; scatter the shredded cheese over the top and cook for a further 4 minutes.
- Slice the omelet into two halves and serve. Bon appétit!

Per serving: 314 Calories; 20.6g Fat; 6.3g Carbs; 23.4g Protein;

86. Elegant Scotch Eggs

(Ready in about 20 minutes | Servings 5)

INGREDIENTS

1/2 cup scallion, finely chopped

2 cloves garlic, minced

Sea salt and ground black pepper, to taste

1 pound ground beef

1 teaspoon hot sauce

1/2 cup almond flour

1 raw egg

3 tablespoons milk

1 ½ cups Parmesan cheese, grated

5 eggs, hard-boiled

DIRECTIONS

- Start by preheating your Air Fryer to 360 degrees F. Mix the scallions, garlic, salt, black pepper, ground beef, and hot sauce; mix until everything is well incorporated.
- Then, create a breading station. In a shallow bowl, place the almond flour. In a second bowl, whisk the raw egg with the milk. Finally, in a third bowl, place the Parmesan cheese.
- Dip each cooked egg in the almond flour mixture. Divide the meat mixture into five balls. Fold them around the hard cooked eggs using your hands.
- Then, dip the eggs into the flour again; dip in the egg/milk mixture. Finally, roll them in the grated cheese to coat on all sides.
- Transfer the scotch eggs to the Air Fryer basket and cook for 16 minutes. Enjoy!

Per serving: 411 Calories; 23.8g Fat; 6g Carbs; 40g Protein;

87. Classic Scrambled Eggs

(Ready in about 15 minutes | Servings 5)

INGREDIENTS

2 tablespoons butter

4 eggs

1/2 teaspoon sea salt

1/4 teaspoon ground black pepper

1/4 teaspoon red pepper flakes

1/2 teaspoon dried parsley flakes

DIRECTIONS

- Start by preheating your Air Fryer to 280 degrees F. Once hot, melt the butter.
- In a mixing bowl, whisk the eggs with the seasonings.
- Cook for 9 to 11 minutes until fluffy and no visible liquid egg remains. Serve warm.

Per serving: 330 Calories; 30.1g Fat; 2g Carbs; 18g Protein;

88. Sunday Two-Cheese Balls

(Ready in about1 hour 15 minutes | Servings 5)

INGREDIENTS

1 ½ cups Colby cheese, preferably
   freshly grated
2 tablespoons almond flour
1 teaspoon granulated garlic

Salt and ground black pepper, to taste
1/2 teaspoon chili flakes
2 eggs
1 ½ cups Parmesan, grated

DIRECTIONS

- Mix the Colby cheese, almond flour, granulated garlic, salt, and black pepper until everything is well incorporated.
- Shape the mixture into bite-size balls and transfer to your freezer for 1 hour.
- Whisk the eggs in a mixing bowl. In another bowl, place the grated parmesan cheese.
- Dip the balls in the beaten eggs. Roll the balls over the Parmesan cheese; arrange the balls on a baking sheet that is lined with a parchment paper.
- Cook at 390 degrees F for 11 minutes; rotating frequently. Bon appétit!

Per serving: 341 Calories; 25.5g Fat; 6.7g Carbs; 21.3g Protein;

89. Cauliflower Mozza Balls

(Ready in about 15 minutes | Servings 4)

INGREDIENTS

1/2 head cauliflower

1/2 cup almond flour

3 ounces mozzarella cheese, shredded

2 eggs

1 teaspoon baking powder

1/2 teaspoon sea salt

1/4 teaspoon ground black pepper

6 tablespoons flaxseed meal

DIRECTIONS

- Pulse your cauliflower in a food possessor until it is well processed.
- Add the flour, cheese, eggs, baking powder, salt, and black pepper; mix until everything is well incorporated.
- Shape this mixture into balls; coat the balls with the flaxseed meal. Cook in the preheated Air Fryer at 390 degrees F for 12 minutes; rotating frequently. Bon appétit!

Per serving: 255 Calories; 19.3g Fat; 5.4g Carbs; 13.4g Protein;

90. Cremini Mushroom Frittata with Cheese

(Ready in about 20 minutes | Servings 2)

INGREDIENTS

1 tablespoon butter

1/2 cup Cremini mushrooms, sliced

1 bell pepper, seeded and chopped

1 serrano pepper, seeded and chopped

4 eggs

1 cup spinach, torn into pieces

Salt and ground black pepper, to taste

3 tablespoons milk

1/4 cup Colby cheese, shredded

DIRECTIONS

- Grease a baking pan with the melted butter. Add the mushrooms and peppers to the pan and cook at 350 degrees F for 6 minutes.
- In a mixing bowl, thoroughly combine the eggs with the spinach, salt, black pepper, and milk. Add the mixture to the pan.
- Top with the cheese and cook an additional 11 minutes. Cut into two slices and serve immediately.

Per serving: 282 Calories; 20.3g Fat; 5.7g Carbs; 17.6g Protein;

91. Two-Cheese and Broccoli Quiche

(Ready in about 45 minutes | Servings 3)

INGREDIENTS

1/2 head broccoli, broken into small florets

1 tomato, chopped

1/2 cup goat cheese, crumbled

1/2 cup sour cream

3 eggs, whisked

1/2 teaspoon smoked paprika

Salt and ground black pepper, to taste

1 cup Swiss cheese, shredded

1 tablespoon fresh chives, chopped

DIRECTIONS

- Steam the broccoli for 18 minutes or until it is tender.
- Then, add the rinsed broccoli to a baking pan that is previously greased with a nonstick cooking spray.
- Add the tomato and goat cheese. In a mixing bowl, thoroughly combine the sour cream with the eggs, paprika, salt, and black pepper.
- Next, pour the egg mixture into the pan. Scatter the shredded Swiss cheese over the top.
- Cook in the preheated Air Fryer at 350 degrees F for 18 to 22 minutes. Serve garnished with fresh chives. Enjoy!

Per serving: 276 Calories; 19g Fat; 6.9g Carbs; 18.3g Protein;

92. Quick and Easy Baked Eggs

(Ready in about 10 minutes | Servings 2)

INGREDIENTS

2 eggs

1/4 teaspoon ground black pepper

1/4 teaspoon salt

1 teaspoon fresh parsley leaves,
   chopped

2 slices of Cheddar cheese

1 tomato, sliced

DIRECTIONS

- Preheat your Air Fryer to 320 degrees F. Spritz 2 ramekins with a nonstick cooking spray.
- Crack an egg into each ramekin; season with black pepper and salt. Bake for 5 to 6 minutes.
- Sprinkle with fresh parsley. Bon appétit!

Per serving: 225 Calories; 19.2g Fat; 4g Carbs; 16.3g Protein;

93. Fried Cheese and Kale Curds

(Ready in about 15 minutes | Servings 4)

INGREDIENTS

- 6 ounces mozzarella cheese
- 1 cup kale, blanched, drained and chopped
- 1/2 cup scallions, chopped
- 2 eggs
- 1/2 teaspoon garlic powder
- 1/2 teaspoon porcini powder
- Kosher salt and ground black pepper, to taste
- 1/4 teaspoon cayenne pepper
- 3 teaspoons flaxseed meal
- 1/2 cup Parmesan cheese, grated

DIRECTIONS

- In a mixing bowl, thoroughly combine all ingredients, except for the Parmesan cheese. Mix until everything is well combined.
- Form into balls and roll into the Parmesan cheese.
- Bake at 350 degrees F for 11 minutes. Serve warm or at room temperature. Enjoy!

Per serving: 284 Calories; 18.7g Fat; 5.6g Carbs; 21.6g Protein;

94. Spicy Ham and Spinach Muffins

(Ready in about 15 minutes | Servings 3)

INGREDIENTS

4 ounces smoked ham, chopped

1 bell pepper, chopped

1 habanero pepper, chopped

1 cup frozen spinach, chopped

4 ounces goat cheese, crumbled

4 eggs, whisked

DIRECTIONS

- Divide the smoked ham, peppers, and spinach between six silicone muffin molds. Add the cheese and whisked eggs.
- Bake at 340 degrees F for 9 minutes. Allow them to cool for 5 minutes before removing from the molds.
- Serve with some extra sour cream or ketchup. Enjoy!

Per serving: 409 Calories; 27.9g Fat; 6.5g Carbs; 32.3g Protein;

95. Vegetarian Cheese-Stuffed Peppers

(Ready in about 15 minutes | Servings 3)

INGREDIENTS

3 bell peppers, deveined and halved

Salt, to taste

1 egg, whisked

6 ounces Ricotta cheese, at room temperature

2 ounces Parmesan cheese, grated

1/2 teaspoon red pepper flakes

DIRECTIONS

- Sprinkle the peppers with salt.
- Mix the egg with the Ricotta cheese; now, divide the Ricotta mixture between the peppers. Top with the Parmesan cheese. Cook at 360 degrees F for 7 minutes.
- Serve at room temperature with a few sprinkles of red pepper flakes. Bon appétit!

Per serving: 223 Calories; 14.2g Fat; 6g Carbs; 14.6g Protein;

96. Mushroom and Blue Cheese Tart

(Ready in about 30 minutes | Servings 4)

INGREDIENTS

4 eggs

1/2 cup heavy cream

1 cup blue cheese, crumbled

1 cup white mushrooms, chopped

1/4 teaspoon salt

1/4 teaspoon ground black pepper

A pinch of grated nutmeg

1/2 cup leeks, chopped

1 garlic clove, smashed

DIRECTIONS

- In a mixing bowl, thoroughly combine the eggs and heavy cream.
- Add the remaining ingredients; mix until everything is well combined. Pour the mixture into a lightly greased baking pan.
- Cook in the preheated Air Fryer at 350 degrees for 28 minutes. Bon appétit!

Per serving: 314 Calories; 25.1g Fat; 4.9g Carbs; 17.4g Protein;

VEGAN

97. Easy Spicy Broccoli

(Ready in about 15 minutes | Servings 4)

INGREDIENTS

1 pound broccoli, cut into florets

2 tablespoons olive oil

1 tablespoon Shoyu sauce

1 teaspoon hot sauce

Salt and ground black pepper, to taste

1 teaspoon paprika

DIRECTIONS

- Preheat your Air Fryer to 395 degrees F. Brush the broccoli florets with olive oil.
- Cook the broccoli for 5 minutes.
- In a mixing bowl, whisk the Shoyu sauce, hot sauce, salt, black pepper, and paprika.
- Toss this sauce with the prepared broccoli and pearl onions. Serve warm, garnished with nutritional yeast.

Per serving: 96 Calories; 8.3g Fat; 4.2g Carbs; 3.8g Protein;

98. Dijon Mashed Rutabaga

(Ready in about 25 minutes | Servings 2)

Per serving: 91 Calories; 4.2g Fat; 6.7g Carbs; 2.3g Protein;

INGREDIENTS

1/2 pound rutabaga, peeled and diced

1 teaspoon sea salt

1/2 teaspoon ground black pepper

1/4 teaspoon smoked paprika

Nonstick cooking spray

1/4 cup soy milk

2 tablespoons vegan margarine

1/2 teaspoon Dijon mustard

1 tablespoon fresh Italian parsley, chopped

DIRECTIONS

- Season the rutabaga with salt, black pepper, and smoked paprika. Spritz your rutabaga with a nonstick cooking spray.
- Cook the seasoned rutabaga for 18 minutes at 400 degrees F.
- Next, mash your rutabaga and add the milk, margarine, and mustard. Mix until everything is well combined.
- Serve garnished with Italian parsley. Bon appétit!

99. Mushroom and Cauliflower Burgers

(Ready in about 35 minutes | Servings 4)

Per serving: 115 Calories; 7.6g Fat; 7g Carbs; 5.7g Protein;

INGREDIENTS

1 tablespoon canola oil

1/2 cup spring onions, finely chopped

1 garlic clove, smashed

1 bell pepper, chopped

1 teaspoon Habanero pepper, chopped

13 ounces mushrooms, chopped into
    small pieces

1/2 head cauliflower, grated

1/2 teaspoon ground cumin

6 tablespoons almond flour

Nonstick cooking spray

DIRECTIONS

- Heat the canola oil in a nonstick skillet that is preheated over a moderate flame.
- Sweat the spring onions and garlic until tender and aromatic. Add the peppers; cook an additional 3 minutes or until tender.
- Now, add the mushrooms and cauliflower; sauté an additional 4 minutes. Add the cumin and almond flour.
- Shape the mixture into patties. Place them in your freezer for 20 minutes.
- Spritz your burgers with a nonstick cooking spray and bake them in the Air Fryer grill pan at 350 degrees F for 10 minutes. Serve with salsa and fresh lettuce. Enjoy!

100. Mushrooms with Sweet and Sour Sauce

(Ready in about 20 minutes | Servings 4)

INGREDIENTS

12 chestnut mushrooms, stalks removed

1 tablespoon olive oil

1/2 small-sized leek, chopped

2 garlic cloves, minced

1 bell pepper, chopped

1 teaspoon cayenne pepper

Sea salt and ground black pepper, to taste

2 tablespoons nutritional yeast flakes

1/2 cup water

1/2 cup tomato puree

1/4 cup Erythritol

1/4 cup seasoned vinegar

DIRECTIONS

- Brush the mushrooms with olive oil. Stuff the mushrooms with the leeks, garlic, and peppers.
- Now, sprinkle them with cayenne pepper, salt, and black pepper. Top with the nutritional yeast flakes.
- Now, cook the stuffed mushrooms in the preheated Air Fryer at 390 degrees F for 11 minutes.
- In a medium pan, simmer the remaining ingredients for the sauce until it has reduced and slightly thickened. Serve the warm mushrooms with sweet and sour sauce on the side. Bon appétit!

Per serving: 130 Calories; 7.3g Fat; 6.5g Carbs; 6.5g Protein;

101. Brussels Sprout Chips

(Ready in about 50 minutes | Servings 4)

INGREDIENTS

1 pound Brussels sprouts, thinly sliced
2 tablespoons olive oil, at room temperature
1/2 teaspoon ground cumin
1 teaspoon garlic powder
1/2 teaspoon salt

DIRECTIONS

- Toss the Brussels sprouts with the olive oil, cumin, garlic powder, and salt.
- Cook at 400 degrees F for 9 minutes, shaking the basket halfway through the cooking time.
- Let it cool before serving time and enjoy!

Per serving: 108 Calories; 7g Fat; 6.1g Carbs; 3.8g Protein;

102. The Best Tofu Ever

(Ready in about 45 minutes | Servings 4)

INGREDIENTS

12 ounces tofu, pressed and cubed

1 tablespoon Shoyu sauce

2 tablespoons tomato puree

1 teaspoon grated ginger, fresh or
   jarred

1 tablespoon olive oil

1 teaspoon dried thyme leaves,
   chopped

2 teaspoons arrowroot starch

4 fresh Boston lettuce leaves

2 medium-sized tomatoes, thinly
   sliced

DIRECTIONS

- Place the tofu in a mixing bowl. Add the Shoyu sauce, tomato puree, ginger, olive oil, and thyme leaves; allow it to marinate for 20 minutes.
- Preheat the Air Fryer to 360 degrees F.
- Then coat the marinated tofu with the arrowroot starch. Cook for 23 minutes, shaking halfway through the cooking time.
- Serve the prepared tofu with the lettuce and tomato slices. Bon appétit!

Per serving: 173 Calories; 10.9g Fat; 5.1g Carbs; 14.1g Protein;

103. Chips with Hot Peanut Butter Sauce

(Ready in about 20 minutes | Servings 2)

INGREDIENTS

3 cups purple kale
2 tablespoons olive oil
Salt, to taste
1/4 cup chunky peanut butter
1 teaspoon soy sauce
1 teaspoon hot sauce

DIRECTIONS

- In a large bowl, toss the kale with the olive oil and salt; transfer to your Air Fryer.
- Cook at 370 degrees F for 5 minutes, shaking halfway through the cooking time.
- In the meantime, make the sauce by mixing the peanut butter, soy sauce, and hot sauce.
- Serve the warm chips with the peanut butter sauce on the side. Bon appétit!

Per serving: 330 Calories; 15.5g Fat; 6.3g Carbs; 10.5g Protein;

104. Spicy Roasted Green Beans

(Ready in about 25 minutes | Servings 4)

INGREDIENTS

10 ounces green beans, canned and
    drained

1 ½ tablespoons dark sesame oil

1/2 teaspoon cayenne pepper

1 teaspoon ground cumin

1 teaspoon chili powder

Salt and ground black pepper, to taste

1 ½ tablespoons lime juice

DIRECTIONS

- Toss the green beans with the remaining ingredients until evenly coated.
- Preheat your Air Fryer to 390 degrees F. Cook green beans for 16 minutes.
- Lower the temperature to 360 degrees F and cook an additional 4 minutes. Enjoy!

Per serving: 68 Calories; 5.4g Fat; 4.6g Carbs; 0.7g Protein;

105. Pad Thai with Vegetable Sauce

(Ready in about 30 minutes | Servings 4)

INGREDIENTS

1/2 head Napa cabbage, shredded

2 tablespoons avocado oil

1/4 cup tamari sauce

1/4 teaspoon blackstrap molasses

1 teaspoon garlic puree

2 tablespoon fresh lime juice

1 bell pepper, chopped

Salt, to taste

1/4 teaspoon ground black pepper

1/4 teaspoon chili powder

1 teaspoon coriander paste

1/2 tablespoon Thai green curry paste

1 (7-ounce) package shirataki fettuccini noodles

2 spring onions, coarsely chopped

DIRECTIONS

- Preheat your Air Fryer to 380 degrees F. Add the shredded cabbage, avocado oil, tamari sauce, molasses, garlic puree and fresh lime juice to the Air Fryer.
- Cook for 10 minutes, shaking halfway through the cooking time.
- Then, add the bell pepper, salt, black pepper, chili powder, and coriander paste.
- Cook for 3 minutes more or until everything is cooked through. Stir in the Thai green curry paste.
- Meanwhile, cook the shirataki noodles until they are soft enough to eat, but still firm. Rinse the noodles and transfer them to a serving bowl.
- Add the cabbage mixture to the bowl; toss to combine and serve garnished with coarsely chopped spring onions.

Per serving: 96 Calories; 7.2g Fat; 6.2g Carbs; 1.5g Protein;

106. Grilled Peppers with Vegan Aioli

(Ready in about 20 minutes | Servings 2)

INGREDIENTS

Nonstick cooking spray

1 orange bell pepper, deveined and cut
　　into four strips lengthwise

1 green bell pepper, deveined and cut
　　into four strips lengthwise

1 sprig thyme, leaves picked

1 sprig rosemary, leaves picked

Flaky salt and ground black pepper, to
　　taste

For Vegan Aioli:

1 small avocado, flesh scooped out

1 teaspoon Dijon mustard

1 tablespoon lemon juice

1/4 teaspoon salt

1/4 teaspoon black pepper

2 tablespoons olive oil

DIRECTIONS

- Give your vegetables a generous spritz with a nonstick cooking spray.
- Sprinkle with the thyme, rosemary, flaky salt and ground black pepper.
- Preheat your Air Fryer to 400 degrees F. Cook the peppers in a grill pan for 12 minutes or until they are softened.
- To make the vegan aioli, add the avocado, mustard, lemon, salt and black pepper to a food processor; blend until well combined.
- With the machine running, pour in the olive oil. Mix until creamy and smooth.
- Serve the grilled tomatoes and peppers with the vegan aioli on the side. Enjoy!

Per serving: 252 Calories; 24.1g Fat; 6.3g Carbs; 2.2g Protein;

107. Mexican Green Beans Ole

(Ready in about 20 minutes | Servings 4)

INGREDIENTS

1 teaspoon garlic powder
1 teaspoon chipotle powder
1/2 teaspoon cumin powder
Salt and red pepper, to taste

1/2 cup almond flour
1 (14.5-ounce) can green beans,
   drained
1/2 avocado, sliced

DIRECTIONS

- Preheat your Air Fryer to 360 degrees F.
- In a mixing bowl, thoroughly combine the garlic powder, chipotle powder, cumin, salt, red pepper, and almond flour.
- Dip the green beans in the flour mixture.
- Cook for 8 minutes, shaking halfway through the cooking time. Serve with the avocado slices. Bon appétit!

Per serving: 135 Calories; 10.1g Fat; 5.7g Carbs; 4.2g Protein;

108. Festive Zucchini Tortillas

(Ready in about 35 minutes | Servings 4)

INGREDIENTS

2 medium-sized zucchinis, grated

2 tablespoons flaxseeds, ground

1 tablespoon psyllium husk

2 tablespoons nutritional yeast

1/4 teaspoon cayenne pepper

Salt, to taste

1/2 cup almond flour

2 tablespoons vegan margarine

DIRECTIONS

- Thoroughly combine all of the above ingredients in a mixing bowl.
- Mix until the batter forms a soft, pliable ball. Divide your batter into four balls.
- Cook at 390 degrees F for 20 minutes, working in batches. Enjoy!

Per serving: 165 Calories; 13.9g Fat; 6.1g Carbs; 5.7g Protein;

109. Asparagus with Green Dip

(Ready in about 25 minutes | Servings 4)

INGREDIENTS

1 pound asparagus spears

1 ½ tablespoons sesame oil

1/2 teaspoon dried basil, crushed

1 teaspoon rosemary, chopped

1/2 teaspoon kosher salt

For the Dipping Sauce:

2 tablespoons watercress

2 tablespoons fresh flat-leaf parsley
  leaves

1 stalk green onion

1/2 cup non-dairy sour cream

1/4 cup vegan mayonnaise

DIRECTIONS

- Begin by preheating your Air Fryer to 360 degrees F.
- Then, toss the asparagus with the sesame oil, basil, rosemary, and salt.
- Cook for 6 minutes without shaking.
- While the asparagus are cooking, prepare the sauce by mixing all of the sauce ingredients in a food processor. Pulse a couple of times or until everything is well incorporated.
- Serve the prepared veggie sticks with the well-chilled dip. Bon appétit!

Per serving: 170 Calories; 14.9g Fat; 6.6g Carbs; 4.4g Protein;

DESSERTS

110. Blood Orange and Ginger Cheesecake

(Ready in about 45 minutes | Servings 10)

INGREDIENTS

1 cup almond flour

1/2 stick butter, melted

7 ounces Neufchatel, at room temperature

1/4 cup sour cream

8 ounces erythritol, powdered

2 eggs

2 tablespoons orange juice

1 teaspoon orange peel, finely shredded

A pinch of salt

A pinch of freshly grated nutmeg

1 teaspoon ground star anise

1/2 teaspoon vanilla paste

2 large blood oranges

2 tablespoons crystallized ginger, finely chopped

DIRECTIONS

- Start by preheating your Air Fryer to 350 degrees F for 5 minutes. Coat the inside of a springform pan with a baking paper.
- Then, in a mixing dish, thoroughly combine the almond flour with the butter. Press this crust into the bottom of a springform pan.
- In a mixing dish, thoroughly combine the Neufchatel with the sour cream and erythritol. Fold in the eggs, one at a time and continue to whisk this mixture.
- Add the orange juice and peel; add all seasonings. Spread this orange layer over the crust in the pan.
- Place the springform pan into your Air Fryer; cook for 13 minutes; then, cook for a further 13 minutes at 320 degrees F,
- Lastly, turn the temperature to 305 degrees F and cook an additional 17 minutes. Garnish with the blood orange and crystallized ginger.
- Refrigerate overnight and serve well-chilled.

Per serving: 201 Calories; 16.4g Fat; 7.1g Carbs; 6.3g Protein;

111. Traditional Tejeringos with Chocolate Sauce

(Ready in about 2 hours 25 minutes | Servings 8)

INGREDIENTS

1 ¼ cups almond flour

1/3 cup erythritol, powdered

1/2 teaspoon baking powder

1 teaspoon baking soda

1/2 teaspoon ground cardamom

1/4 teaspoon crystallized ginger

1/8 teaspoon grated nutmeg

A pinch of salt

1 egg white

1/3 cup ghee, melted

1/3 cup evaporated milk

For the Chocolate Sauce:

3 ounces cocoa powder, no sugar added

1 ounce coconut oil

1/2 cup heavy cream

DIRECTIONS

- Thoroughly combine the almond flour, erythritol, baking powder, baking soda, cardamom, ginger, nutmeg, and salt in a mixing bowl.
- Fold in the egg white, ghee, and milk, and whisk with a fork.
- Transfer the dough to your refrigerator for 2 hours. Cover the bottom of your Air Fryer with a sheet of baking paper.
- Knead the dough and transfer it to a pastry bag fitted with a large star tip. Pipe 4-inch long strips of dough into the cooking basket, without crowding; spritz with a nonstick cooking oil.
- Air fry at 365 degrees F for 7 minutes.
- To make the sauce, in a small-sized pan, warm the cocoa powder, coconut oil, and heavy cream. Serve the prepared Tejeringos with the chocolate sauce. Bon appétit!

Per serving: 175 Calories; 14.4g Fat; 6.4g Carbs; 3.3g Protein;

112. Sunday Berry Cobbler

(Ready in about 20 minutes | Servings 2)

INGREDIENTS

1 cups mixed berries

1/4 cup swerve

2 tablespoons butter, melted

1/4 teaspoon grated nutmeg

1/2 teaspoon ground cinnamon

1/3 teaspoon ground star anise

A pinch of coarse salt

1/3 cup almond flour

2 tablespoons coconut oil, room temperature

DIRECTIONS

- Start by preheating your Air Fryer to 360 degrees F for 5 minutes.
- Toss the apple slices with the swerve, butter, nutmeg, cinnamon, star anise, and salt. Top with the almond flour mixed with the coconut oil.
- Cook for 14 minutes, shaking halfway through the cooking time.
- Store in an airtight container and enjoy!

Per serving: 326 Calories; 32.5g Fat; 6.5g Carbs; 3.6g Protein;

113. Winter Fruit and Nut Dessert

(Ready in about 45 minutes | Servings 5)

INGREDIENTS

Nonstick cooking spray

2 cups blueberries

1/2 cup walnuts, ground

3/4 cup swerve

1/2 teaspoon ground cinnamon

3 teaspoons coconut oil, cold

1 cup heavy cream

DIRECTIONS

- Begin by preheating your Air Fryer to 370 degrees F. Lightly spritz a baking pan with a nonstick cooking oil.
- Now, add a layer of blueberries. Sprinkle with the walnuts, swerve, and cinnamon; repeat until you run out of ingredients.
- Crumb the coconut oil over the top and bake for 35 minutes or until syrupy. Allow it to sit at room temperature until it is firm enough to slice.
- Serve at room temperature, topped with heavy cream. Bon appétit!

Per serving: 155 Calories; 12.6g Fat; 6.1g Carbs; 2.8g Protein;

115. Chocolate and Pecan Cupcakes

(Ready in about 25 minutes | Servings 12)

INGREDIENTS

1/2 cup almond flour

1/2 teaspoon baking powder

2 tablespoons evaporated milk

1 stick butter, at room temperature

1/3 cup swerve

1/4 teaspoon cardamom

1/4 teaspoon grated nutmeg

2 tablespoons pecans, chopped

2 ounces low-carb chocolate chips

DIRECTIONS

- Preheat your Air Fryer to 320 degrees F. Grease a muffin tin with a nonstick cooking spray.
- In a mixing bowl, sift the almond flour and baking powder.
- In another bowl, thoroughly combine the milk with the butter, swerve, cardamom, and nutmeg. Fold in the chopped pecans and chocolate chips.
- Divide the mixture among the muffin cups and transfer to your Air Fryer. Bake for 12 minutes.
- Turn off your Air Fryer and let the cupcakes sit for 8 minutes. Unmold your cupcakes and transfer them to a dessert platter. Bon appétit!

Per serving: 132 Calories; 10.8g Fat; 6.8g Carbs; 1.3g Protein;

116. Grandma's Butter Rum Cookies

(Ready in about 25 minutes | Servings 10)

INGREDIENTS

1 cup almond flour

1 cup coconut flour

1 packet baking powder

1/2 teaspoon sea salt

1 stick butter, at room temperature

1 cup swerve

2 tablespoons buttermilk

2 tablespoons rum

1/2 teaspoon butter rum flavoring

2 ounces walnuts, finely chopped

DIRECTIONS

- Begin by preheating the Air Fryer to 360 degrees F for 5 to 10 minutes.
- In a mixing dish, thoroughly combine the flour with the baking powder and sea salt.
- Beat the butter and swerve with a hand mixer until pale and fluffy. Now, stir in the flour mixture.
- Add the remaining ingredients; mix to combine well. Divide the mixture into 14 small balls; flatten each ball with a fork and transfer them to a foil-lined baking pan.
- Put the baking pan into the Air Fryer and bake your cookies for 14 minutes. Work in a few batches, without crowding. Bon appétit!

Per serving: 211 Calories; 20.5g Fat; 4.2g Carbs; 3.3g Protein;

117. Heavenly Chocolate Cake

(Ready in about 25 minutes | Servings 8)

INGREDIENTS

1/2 cup erythritol, powdered

1 stick butter, at room temperature

2 eggs, beaten

1 cup almond flour

1 teaspoon baking powder

2 teaspoons raw cocoa powder

1/2 teaspoon vanilla essence

1/8 teaspoon salt

1/8 teaspoon grated nutmeg

2 ounces unsweetened baker's chocolate

1 tablespoon heavy cream

1/4 cup fresh raspberries, to decorate

DIRECTIONS

- Begin by preheating your Air Fryer to 320 degrees F. Spritz the inside of a baking pan with a nonstick cooking spray.
- Now, beat the erythritol and butter with an electric mixer until the mixture is creamy. Fold in the eggs and mix again.
- Then, add the flour, baking powder, cocoa powder, vanilla, salt, and nutmeg. Afterwards, stir in the chocolate and heavy cream; mix to combine well.
- Scrape the batter into the prepared baking pan and level the surface using a spatula.
- Bake for 16 minutes or until a tester inserted in the center of your cake comes out dry. Decorate with fresh raspberries, cut into slices, and enjoy!

Per serving: 185 Calories; 15.9g Fat; 5.5g Carbs; 6.4g Protein;

118. Best Ever Zucchini Cake

(Ready in about 40 minutes | Servings 8)

INGREDIENTS

1 ¼ cups coconut flour
1 ½ teaspoons baking powder
1/2 teaspoon salt
4 tablespoons coconut oil
1/2 cup erythritol
2 eggs
1 zucchini
1/3 teaspoon cardamom
1/2 teaspoon ground star anise

For the Frosting:
2 ounces cream cheese
1/2 cup powdered erythritol
1 tablespoon butter, softened
2 tablespoons milk

DIRECTIONS

- Start by preheating the Air Fryer to 325 degrees F for 5 minutes. Now, brush a baking pan with a butter-flavored nonstick cooking spray.
- In a mixing dish, thoroughly combine the coconut flour with the baking powder and salt.
- Beat the coconut oil and erythritol until the mixture is smooth and uniform. Stir in the eggs and zucchini; mix again to combine well.
- Add the flour mixture, along with the cardamom and anise. Mix again.
- Spoon the batter into the baking pan. Transfer to the preheated Air Fryer and bake for 35 minutes. Transfer to a wire rack to cool completely.
- Meanwhile, make the frosting by mixing the remaining ingredients. Frost your cake and enjoy!

Per serving: 133 Calories; 12.6g Fat; 5.1g Carbs; 3.2g Protein;

119. Sponge Cake with Cherry Curd

(Ready in about 1 hour | Servings 10)

INGREDIENTS

Nonstick cooking spray
1 ½ sticks butter
1 1/3 cup erythritol
2 eggs
1 cup almond flour
1/2 teaspoon baking powder
1/2 teaspoon ground star anise
1 teaspoon vanilla extract

For the Filling:
2 eggs, whisked
1 tablespoon fresh lemon juice
1/4 teaspoon crystallized ginger
1 cup erythritol
8 ounces cherries, pitted
1 ½ ounces butter, unsalted

DIRECTIONS

- Begin by preheating your Air Fryer to 360 degrees F. Then spritz two baking pans with a nonstick cooking spray.
- Beat 1 ½ sticks of butter and 1 1/3 cup of erythritol until the mixture is creamy and fluffy. Crack the eggs in and continue to mix until pale and smooth.
- Now, sift in the flour; add the baking powder, star anise, and vanilla extract.
- Scrape the batter into the prepared baking pan and bake for 15 minutes. Turn the temperature to 340 degrees F and bake for a further 10 minutes or until a skewer inserted into the middle of your cake comes out dry.
- Allow it to cool on a wire rack. Repeat with another cake.
- Place a glass bowl over a pot of boiling water. Add the whisked eggs, lemon juice, ginger, and 1 cup erythritol; mix to combine.
- Now, add the cherries and 1 ½ ounces of unsalted butter to the bowl, stirring constantly about 18 minutes. The curd will harden as it cools.
- Place the first cake on a serving platter. Spread the filling over the cake and then, top with the other cake. Bon appétit!

Per serving: 254 Calories; 24.7g Fat; 4.4g Carbs; 5.2g Protein;

120. Christmas Mint Chocolate Cake

(Ready in about 20 minutes | Servings 10)

INGREDIENTS

1 cup almond flour

1/2 cup coconut flour

1 ½ teaspoons baking powder

1/2 teaspoon kosher salt

1 ½ cups powdered erythritol

2 tablespoons raw cocoa powder

1 stick butter

2 eggs

3 tablespoons double cream

1/2 teaspoon mint extract

1 ounce baking chocolate, chopped
  into chunks

DIRECTIONS

- Begin by preheating your Air Fryer to 360 degrees F. Lightly grease a baking pan.
- In a mixing bowl, thoroughly combine the flour, baking powder, and salt. Add the powdered erythritol and cocoa; mix to combine.
- Cut in the butter and stir again.
- In another bowl, mix the eggs with the double cream; add this mixture to the bowl with the flour mixture.
- Lastly, add the mint extract and chocolate; mix to combine well. Scrape the batter into the prepared baking pan.
- Bake for 10 minutes or until a skewer inserted into the middle of your cake comes out dry. Bon appétit!

Per serving: 214 Calories; 17.1g Fat; 4.5g Carbs; 3.6g Protein;

Made in the USA
Coppell, TX
29 October 2019